An Exceptional Life

A STORY OF FAITH, MISSING CHROMOSOMES & UNCONDITIONAL LOVE

Jada L. Babcock

NEW HARBOR PRESS

RAPID CITY, SD

Babcock/New Harbor Press
1601 Mt. Rushmore Rd, Ste 3288
Rapid City, SD 57701
www.NewHarborPress.com

Ordering Information:
Quantity sales. Special discounts are available on quantity purchases by corporations, associations, and others. For details, contact the "Special Sales Department" at the address above.

An Exceptional Life / Jada L. Babcock. -- 1st ed.
ISBN 978-1-63357-386-4

Contents

Introduction

COLEMAN BABCOCK ENTERED THE world on February 17, 2012, after an uneventful pregnancy and easy birth. Soon after his arrival and in dramatic fashion, he was rushed to the Neonatal Intensive Care Unit for emergency medical intervention. Not expecting anything other than a healthy newborn, the reality I was handed that day wrapped in the drab hospital-issued blanket shattered all the hopes and dreams I had for him, along with my heart. Once released from the hospital nearly two weeks later, he endured numerous genetic tests and specialist visits while we searched for answers. At fourteen months old, he was finally diagnosed with an extremely rare Chromosome 13q Deletion, one of only five people in the world to have such a diagnosis.

Has life ever thrown you a curveball, creating chaos, uncertainty, and doubt? How hard is it to find the good when everything seems to be falling apart? Do you ever feel alone, like no one understands your struggles and pain?

When our life with Coleman didn't start out as planned, anxiety and fear consumed me. There was no *What to Expect* handbook for our child because he was different from the rest. People would try to comfort and support us, but how could they possibly know what we were going through? I craved to have a connection with another family that understood the daily struggles, but also knew how rewarding this life could be! I longed to see evidence that my child wasn't a burden as the world described him but was instead a gift with incredible value from a loving Heavenly Father.

I started writing *An Exceptional Life: A Story of Faith, Missing Chromosomes & Unconditional Love* as a way to dig down deep into the dark, dank corners of our story and shine a light on the blessings that were buried under the hurt. Based on my personal journals and handwritten letters, the book dives into the real, raw emotions as well as the amazing joy that accompanies raising a child with special needs. When I focused on the pain of life right in front of me, I often missed the goodness that was there all along.

Through prayer and studying God's word, I worked through processing grief, blame, and then eventual acceptance of who God had created my son to be.

Coleman's challenges and successes give him daily opportunities to show God's love and faithfulness to everyone he encounters.

The undeniable, never-ending hope that God provides during storms is evident throughout our story, and as you turn each page, I pray that you will begin to seek out the blessings in your own life. Although the narrative is specific to our situation, the underlying themes of searching for hope when life seems hopeless, rejoicing during heartbreak, and fully relinquishing control over to God, are relatable to anyone, regardless of the season you are walking through.

At the end of each chapter, you have the opportunity to reflect and journal your own experiences, whether related to raising a child with special needs or not. Several prompts are included on each journal page to help guide you, or you can write freely what is on your mind and in your heart.

These personal reflections can be reread at later times as proof of your survival during great suffering and a testament of God's grace and love. As Christians, we are not promised a life without trials or trauma, but by reflecting on what we have gone through and the truths we find in scripture, we can see what God has done amid those gut-wrenching moments.

I invite you to come along with us on this difficult but beautiful life with our extraordinary Coleman. May our journey provide you comfort, encouragement, and hope as you navigate your own.

CHAPTER 1

Welcome to the World

"Welcome to the world, my sweet, little Coleman. As I look down at your perfect little squishy face and round, pouty lips, you have given me a new perspective on what is truly important in life. With all the unknowns right now, there is one thing that is known and will never change: my love for you! I admit that I am scared (terrified, really) of being your mommy. What if I am not enough? Although I am sure I will fail at times, I promise to try my best to give you everything you need, protect you from the harshness of the world, and be there to dry your tears when life gets tough. You have value and a purpose here on earth. I am anxious to watch you grow and change and see God's plan for you unfold."

ALL STORIES HAVE A beginning. Some are profound and exciting while others are traumatic and unexpected. Occasionally, you run across a few that are an amalgamation of all these characteristics and emotions. No two beginnings are the same, nor are the stories and experiences that follow, but somehow, they draw us to one another in ways we don't fully comprehend. The connections we make aren't coincidental but are masterfully planned and purposefully put into action by a loving Heavenly Father.

Our stories can be hard to share at times because they cause us to dig deep and face head-on the failures, grief, and pain that are lurking in the valleys of our lives. We shouldn't let the hurt shield our souls to the point where we are unable to look back and see mountains being moved. The pivotal periods of time when impossible became possible, and God's hand in our lives is evident every step of the way. Through His strength and grace, we can pick ourselves up, dust ourselves off, and keep moving forward. Our struggles and triumphs both reflect His faithfulness and unconditional love and can provide the perfect opportunities to share Him with others.

So here I am, sharing our story with you. The good, bad, and ugly. The brokenness and tears. The joy and healing. Our beginning. The day Coleman Luke came into our lives and changed everything. How could someone so small make such a huge impact?

Walking down the long hospital hallway towards the birthing suite at an hour when most of the city was still sleeping, Mike and I were faced with the enormity of our situation and its magnitude started to slowly sink in. We had toured this very room when we attended the free birthing classes a couple of months prior. The classes are educational in nature and help provide new parents a sense of security that they are prepared for anything that might arise. Although I had been there before, the room seemed eerily unfamiliar and sterile. The coldness gave me a chill.

My emotions and anxieties began to overwhelm me. My mind wasn't present and coherent but was busy jumping from one unlikely scenario to another. I was so distracted that I put my hospital gown on backwards. The first step of the birthing process, and I had already failed. After a sweet nurse pointed out my hospital fashion faux pas, I adjusted the generic-looking grey gown to its proper placement. Once all my undergarments and the remainder of any sense of modesty had been removed, heart monitors were wrapped around my bulging baby bump to check the baby's heart rhythm.

I was being induced at forty-one weeks after an easy, uneventful pregnancy. Other than a little morning sickness during my first trimester, I had no major issues. I ate right, exercised, and took all my prenatal vitamins.

All my lab work came back normal, including the genetic tests. The ultrasound from my 20-week appointment showed no abnormalities but did confirm our hopes that our first born would be male. All was right with the center of our universe.

Watching the rhythm of my baby's heartbeat on the monitor was almost cathartic. My anxiousness melted away and the realization that we would be meeting him in a few short hours led to feelings of genuine excitement. This was it. Game day. The day we had planned for and anticipated for over nine months.

My airy, dreamlike state of relaxation was abruptly suspended when the delivery nurse came in to check the heart rate monitor. She mumbled something under her breath. It was probably nothing important I told myself and quickly disregarded any concern as she left the room.

We had been waiting about an hour for something, anything to happen. Mike was lounging on the plastic couch flipping mindlessly through the channels on the television set. Trying to find something that would pique our interest and take our minds off the impatience that was starting to build in both of us.

The nurse came back in after what felt like an eternity and walked briskly to the monitor to observe. She pointed to a little section of squiggles that had penetrated the boundaries of the parallel lines that indicated "normal." Some squiggles were above the top line while others fell below the bottom line. "The baby's heart rate is a little inconsistent, but it doesn't necessarily mean anything is wrong," she stated. She informed us that she wanted to watch it for a little while longer and make sure it stabilized before starting the induction. Eventually, Coleman's heart began co-operating, so the medication was started around 7:30 a.m.

Childbirth has been described as a beautiful experience by mothers for generations. A more accurate description from my personal experience would be messy, raw, powerful, painful, exhausting, gross, and miraculous. All the adjectives in the English language couldn't accurately capture the essence of bringing a child into the world. After a much-appreciated epidural and three pushes later, our Coleman had arrived. His birth couldn't have been more perfect had it been scripted from a medical textbook. The child looked identical to his father except for his awkwardly shaped feet. Those feet were my contribution to the creation of this precious life.

Seven pounds and ten ounces, our screaming boy let his presence be known as he left the comfort and warmth of my womb. He was immediately placed on my breast, as nurses wiped his eyes and nose clean. When our eyes locked, he settled down like he knew I was going to protect him from any harm that might come his way. Mike was standing over us crying (hopefully from the happiness of meeting his firstborn and not from the trauma of watching the actual birthing process). Whatever the reason for the tears, it was a powerfully, moving memory that I will cherish forever.

As I was being tended to by my ob-gyn, Coleman was being evaluated, measured, and supplied a little burst of oxygen to get the lungs kicked into high gear, although it was already apparent to everyone in the room that they were working just fine. Nothing was amiss. Nothing raised red flags. He was flipped this way and that and swaddled in such a manner that only professionals who have been handling newborn babies for twenty-five years knew how. Once again, he was placed upon my chest. The nurses exited the room with the intent of returning half an hour later to take him to the well-baby nursery for more poking and prodding and to meet his new pediatrician.

We were now a family of three. Hopes and dreams for the future and excitement to see how he would take after each of us filled our conversations. All my anxiety from that morning was for naught since he was healthy, happy, and safely in my arms. One of the nurses returned and asked Mike to carry him down the hall to the nursery. "He has a large fan club out there and they have been waiting patiently to meet him," the nurse said. Off walked my entire world, one piece of my heart cradling another. Grandparents, cousins, aunts, and uncles all crowded around, as Coleman proceeded to greet his admirers on the way to the nursery. Snapping pictures as they "Oohed" and "Aahed." Capturing a proud Papa, grinning ear to ear, showing off his new cub.

Mike returned a short while later with the update that he had made it safely to the well-baby nursery with no issues. I'm not sure what we thought might happen, but it was still reassuring to hear he had been safely handed off. As we chatted and waited patiently on a recovery room vacancy, the nurse stepped back in and asked Mike to return to the nursery with her to fill out some forms. A different nurse came in and said a room had become available so she would wheel me in my hospital bed to the other wing. Mike and Coleman would come meet up with me there later.

He had been born at 3:00 p.m., and although time seemed to fly by, I was still surprised when I looked out the window and it was completely dark. How long had Mike been gone? Why were none of our other family members coming to my room to visit? Where was my baby? I can't explain it or truly understand it, but I knew in my gut that something was wrong with him.

Something was terribly wrong. Either it was my new-found maternal instinct, God preparing me for the news I was about to hear, or both, I just knew. Alone in my panic, I went through all the possibilities that I could fathom, but none eased my sense of uneasiness. He was probably just jaundice and needed to be under an UV light for a few hours or his sugars might be out of whack and needed monitoring. Trying to minimize a situation that you know down to your core is going to be life-changing is a very pointless process.

Slowly, the creaking door of the hospital room swung open as Mike walked towards me. When I looked up at him, my suspicions were immediately confirmed. Through tears, he blurted out in one breath, "Something is wrong with Coleman and they don't know what it is, maybe Down Syndrome or something like that, and they are taking him to the Neonatal Intensive Care Unit." He slowly exhaled as he walked over and held my hand. I was light-headed and shaking. Tears formed in my eyes but wouldn't fall. I may have been trying to be strong for Mike or my body could have been in shock from the news, but I felt utterly numb. Mike said when he walked back down the hallway towards the nursery to fill out the forms, all our family members had somber looks on their faces. The curtains had been drawn on the nursery observation windows, and you could hear a pin drop. As he entered the nursery, his first impression was that Coleman was dead. He was a purplish-blue color and was lethargic with his new pediatrician standing next to him looking concerned.

A knock at the door interrupted Mike's emotional retelling of the events that had transpired. In walked the pediatrician and my ob-gyn. The pediatrician rushed to my bedside and grabbed my hand, while the ob-gyn stood supportively at the foot of the bed. With tears in her eyes, the pediatrician said, "There are some physical abnormalities that could be markers of a chromosome issue, so we are going to run some tests to check for conditions like Down Syndrome. The reason Coleman is going to the NICU is because his body isn't making platelets, so he is bruised from the birthing process and could possibly have some internal bleeding. He is stable right now and you will get to see him soon. We will take the best care of your little one." The compassion that was shown by both doctors will forever set the standard to which I hold all medical professionals. I needed real, raw emotions instead of vague clinical explanations. I needed the tears with the facts and the hugs and assurances that we would all work together to get answers to help him survive.

After the doctors exited, our family began trickling in a couple at a time to cry, give hugs, and say prayers.

They all eventually left to begin spreading the news down the pipeline so church prayer chains could be activated and everyone who was interested could have the latest news on "Baby Cole." In the quietness of the room, Mike and I found ourselves trying to comprehend and cope with all the activity from the last few hours. All I wanted to do was hold my baby again, touch his face, whisper "I love you," and make sure he knew he wasn't alone.

My determination to be reunited with Coleman finally paid off and around 10:00 p.m., the nurse told us that we could go to the NICU to see him. Because I had an epidural, they wouldn't let me walk the distance to the NICU and insisted on pushing me in a wheelchair. This minor inconvenience caused major frustration because although logical—I understood there are policies in place to protect the hospital from being liable if I fell—I felt it was just another barrier costing me precious seconds with my child. I wanted to scream, shout, and spew the anger that was building inside me at every soul that passed by. My perception of the situation was that no one cared about the very real possibility that my baby was dying all alone in a NICU pod.

As I was wheeled up to the open bed and handed Coleman, an impenetrable guard went up around my heart. A steel reinforced, concrete barrier that was so well built, a beam of light couldn't even shine its way through. It sounds terrible and took me a long time to admit it, but it was one of my subconscious, ill-advised coping mechanisms. Because of the trauma we had just experienced, it was the only way I knew how to exist. And that was all I was doing at that point—existing. I was present in body playing the role of a mother, but secretly, I had placed the parts of my reality that were too hard to process into a tiny box and tucked it away to be dealt with later.

The fear of possibly losing my child took control of me. If I didn't love him completely with my whole heart, it wouldn't hurt as bad if he was taken away from me. I have tears in my eyes as I write this because what decent mother could feel such a way? I would have died for him in that moment, but the feelings of joy and happiness experienced in the delivery room were no longer present. The contradiction was so confusing and was continuously fueled by my anxiety, new-mom hormones, and the unknowns. Everything became a blur yet was still so crystal clear. A perfect storm brewing and building waiting to cause irreparable harm to my mental health.

Through many tears and prayers, I was slowly able to take the wall down piece by piece. My baby needed me to love him without stipulation; without holding back because of what might happen or because I didn't think I was strong enough to face the hardest of outcomes. This truth hit me like a tsunami, literally knocking the air from my lungs. God had brought this child into the world for a purpose, and regardless of the fear and heartache we were facing being his parents, they paled in comparison to the struggles and pain he was facing at only a few hours old. If he died, he would know nothing but love from us. If he lived, he would know nothing but love from us. He deserved unconditional love... and we deserved the chance to give it to him.

> **"The Lord is near to the brokenhearted**
> **and saves the crushed in spirit."**
> *Psalm 34:18 (ESV)*

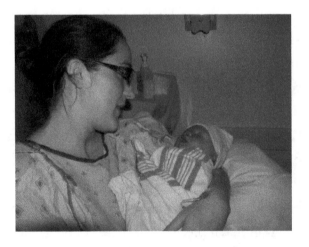

Personal Reflections

What unexpected events have caused you to want to detach from your reality and put up a wall to protect yourself from possible heartache? What emotions did you feel and how did you cope? How was your faith affected by the experience?

CHAPTER 2

Grief and Understanding

"My heart is breaking as I look at you all hooked up to machines. You seem so vulnerable, so tiny, but I can see that spark of fight in your eyes when you peek up at me. You will give it 110%, and I promise you we will do the same. We don't know how long God will allow you to stay with us, but while you are ours, you will never, ever experience a day without love. I wish I could take away all your pain and struggles. My prayers are filled with nothing but you as I cry out for peace and understanding. My dreams are troubled with all the things that could go wrong, but when you are in my arms, the load of my distress lightens tremendously. We are in this battle together, kid, and you will never have to fight alone."

THE WING OF THE hospital that housed the Neonatal Intensive Care Unit was reminiscent of a high-security prison; not in its appearance necessarily, but in its ability to make a person feel isolated and confined. Scrubbing my skin raw up to the elbow with the aromatic disinfecting soap and dressing in the sterile yellow gown became almost a reflex, an innate behavior that was performed without thought or awareness.

Peeking into the clear plastic domes that protected the most fragile of humans from the dangers of a world they weren't ready to live in, I see the tiny bodies fighting with every ounce of their strength to survive. Their skin translucent, revealing the circulatory highways busy pumping the life-giving blood and oxygen to their barely formed hearts and lungs. Defying science and baffling medical professionals. Some of these babies will live their entire lives in this unit, it being the only earthly home they will ever know. Others will call it home for weeks or months before being paroled to begin their lives on the outside. Freedom is the ultimate outcome for all the NICU families, and ours was no exception.

We live in an era of modern medicine, where childbirth isn't as dangerous as it was a hundred years ago. Medical conditions are caught early and treated with technology that would have been considered science fiction a few decades back. The knowledge of genetics has grown so much recently that there seems to be a feeling of complacency in the ability to identify abnormalities and diagnose conditions quickly. Because these scientific advances are wonderful and amazing and have saved so many lives, it is easy to overlook the potential that this very science can also deliver a devastating diagnosis that will shake you to your core.

Next to the other residents of the NICU, Coleman looked like an average, healthy newborn. The bruising slowly faded, and his skin returned to its original peachy hue because his body began manufacturing the platelets he so desperately needed. Only the wires to his heart rate and pulse ox monitors were left connected. To the casual observer, his seemingly healthy appearance made him look out of place in the specialty unit, but the decision to place him in there was still very much warranted.

Because of my decision to love him fully without hesitation, the grief that I had so neatly packaged and shoved down deep inside came rushing to the surface and bubbling over like hot lava from a newly awakened volcano. The pain was nearly unbearable, and I could feel the sting from my wounded heart each time it beat.

It seems odd to grieve someone who has not died. He was still very much alive, yet the anguish I was experiencing was comparable to moments when death had come for a visit. The truth is, I wasn't grieving the child that I had been given, but rather the idea of the child that I had daydreamed about since I was a little girl playing with dolls. I wasn't sad because my child would never be an astronaut or play college sports, but because I had those dreams of the future without the realization that he may never walk, talk, or live independently.

Unless they are in the trenches with you, explaining the sorrow to outsiders is extremely difficult, if not impossible. How could they understand the pain associated with the loss of something so abstract? How could you explain the concept when you truly don't understand it yourself? My assumption that Coleman would follow a typical developmental path and easily meet milestones within the parameters specified by the medical community prevented me from realizing that there was even an alternative. Our newly discovered slap-in-the-face, punch-in-the-gut reality was that he may not be able to reach any of the milestones, ever. He could be forever stranded, all alone, on the shoulder of the typical path, watching his peers pass him by one by one. Although certain literature provided me with optimistic expectations of the future prior to his birth, it was now very clear that those expectations were not applicable to our situation.

Anxiety has tortured me for as long back as I can remember. When I was growing up, a constant ball of adult-like worry held me captive within my small frame. During certain situations when I was unable to hide my distress, such as school, my parents helped me identify my triggers and arranged extra support to be available, if needed. I developed ingenious coping strategies, but when life got to be too overwhelming, I was perceived as overly emotional or temperamental. Anxiety, my old nemesis, had caused me to miss opportunities, lose friends, and be labeled as weird and socially awkward. As I became an adult, I was finally brave enough to speak to my doctor and get a prescription for anti-anxiety medicine. I unashamedly accepted the fact that my brain doesn't produce the chemicals needed to keep the anxiety in-check, so I require medication to fill in the missing pieces.

For years, my anxiety was fairly well-managed with only a few hiccups along the way. Due to risks associated with the medication during pregnancy, I had opted to stop it completely when Mike and I decided to start our family. I managed the pregnancy like a champ, being no more anxious than most first-time moms-to-be and handling the fears that I did encounter in healthy, natural ways.

After Coleman's birth, however, my emotional and physical well-being took a most ominous turn. I couldn't eat more than a few bites of my hospital-issued meals without vomiting or sleep more than half an hour without startling myself awake. My body felt as if it would completely shut down from the strain it was under. I had gained forty pounds during my pregnancy and had lost thirty thirteen days later when he was discharged from the NICU. Even through the unintentional purging of my body and insomnia that ensued, I continued producing an abundance of breastmilk to nourish my baby. He was unable to latch at the breast, but I was able to pump a hearty supply that kept his little tummy fed and happy. Pumping gave me a task to focus on instead of the rotating, irrational storylines that played on repeat in my mind. The respite was short-lived because, as soon as I was done pumping and feeding him, my mind would return to chaos.

Anxiety attacks were stealing my ability to function normally and destroying any ounce of joy that had remained. I was unable to care for myself, but now I was expected to be responsible for making life or death decisions for my baby. I had fallen overboard and was slowly slipping under the waves, desperately fighting for air but losing the battle.

As if she heard my silent, dejected cries for help, the hospital social worker appeared out of thin air to see if we needed assistance. She was an amazingly soft-spoken woman who looked like an angel dressed in white scrubs. She listened and nodded with expressions of empathy and understanding. She spoke thoughtful words of validation and encouragement. She gifted us a small blue-covered notebook, the kind you find in the discount bin of an office supply store and told us to write down everything. Everything we heard, felt, saw, and experienced during our stay at the hospital. From doctors' notes to visitor logs; from our emotions to our greatest fears. It was all to be recorded in our new journal.

Some days, I wrote one word as that is all that I had in me to describe how I felt. Other days I wrote a short novel. By journaling, our lives became manageable. It also gave us a record of everything that happened during his NICU stay, which became a tremendous help as we began seeing specialists and therapists after he was discharged. Our sleep-deprived brains couldn't comprehend and retain the plethora of information that bombarded us daily, much less regurgitate it on cue with any accuracy. That little notebook was a lifesaver, a flotation device that kept me from drowning.

Time is such a precious gift. People cling to it and savor the goodness of life out of every drop, never knowing when it will run out for good. In the hospital, the concept of time became a direct contradiction to how I had always viewed it. It was now an impossible feat that had to be conquered, a test of survival for my sanity.

By breaking the days into small increments of time, I was able to mentally make it through without becoming overwhelmed by the unknowns that laid waiting in the hours ahead. Surviving one minute at a time, celebrating my success, and then trying to get through the next. Eventually, the minutes turned to hours and the hours turned to days, and survival came as second nature, with much less effort and heartache.

The initial genetic testing had been completed within a few hours after birth, and the results had been returned with no discrepancies. Coleman was now considered a medical conundrum with the doctors stepping in to fill the role of super sleuths, ready to crack the case.

We live in Louisiana where Mardi Gras is an adored and much anticipated time of celebration and fun. The carnival season is part of the culture and it frequently shuts down main thoroughfares, so parade floats can maneuver through cities and towns. Schools and businesses close, so young and old alike can revel in the festivities. Unfortunately, Coleman was born on the Friday before Fat Tuesday, so most of the medical community had followed the trend and closed-up shop. Delays became the norm and answers were few and far between. After a bit of intense encouragement from an exhausted, extremely frustrated Mike, the hospital eventually called in staff after hours to begin running scans and tests from the top of Coleman's head to the bottom of his tiny feet.

Their objective was to discover if any internal issues were present, in addition to his physical traits, that could facilitate in identifying his mysterious syndrome. I dreaded getting results, but I dreaded ignorance more. The quest for a diagnosis felt like nothing other than an interrogation and the questions fired at us, although necessary for the doctors to rule out certain causes, created an entirely new fear. What if one of us had done something or were exposed to something that had caused his issues?

Some medical professionals that we encountered chose to handle our case using a detached, impersonal approach, far removed from the emotions and suffering involved. Coleman was a case study and nothing more. They used the guise of science to fulfill their own curiosities, and the manner in which they engaged us contained zero empathy or genuine concern. As distraught, desperate parents we were hoping for some answers or in the very least, some guesses, but instead, the barrage of questions created nothing but feelings of guilt and anger.

The first question that was thrown at us was, "Are you and the father related?" Well, to be honest, that had never crossed my mind as even something we should verify. I was 99.9 percent sure that we were not related, but that question raised a 0.1 percent sliver of doubt in my anxiety-riddled mind. I mean, I have never seen him at a family reunion and there is no one with that last name anywhere in my family tree, but I do have fourth cousins that are redheaded that live around where he is from . . . so maybe . . . Luckily, during the process, we did in fact confirm that we are not related. That would have been an unwelcome plot twist after seven years of marriage.

"Were you sick during your pregnancy? Did you take any medications or use drugs or alcohol? Were you exposed to any chemicals?" followed the initial question in quick, rapid-fire succession. Mike worked for a crop-dusting company and was around different kinds of pesticides and herbicides. Could one of my visits during my early pregnancy expose me to something even though I was very, very careful and stayed away from the spray sites? I had acne in high school and took medicine that was known to cause birth defects. Maybe there were residual effects from that medication even though research disputed that claim. I didn't use drugs or alcohol, but maybe I took too many prenatal vitamins or not enough. A black hole of guilt opened up, and I kept falling deeper and deeper into the dark abyss of blame.

Spiritually, I felt that God was punishing me for a sin from my past, and my child was forced to pay my dues. Taking an inventory of every sin I had ever committed in my life was a tad bit time-consuming and caused me to dig up the once dirty rags that Jesus had already washed white as snow. With his confident, manipulative whispers, Satan kept reminding me how unworthy and broken I was. The seed of guilt was planted and as it grew, it obstructed my eyes, so I was unable to see the blessing that God had given me in Coleman. In contrast, Mike became angry at God. His faith was tested tremendously, and he couldn't comprehend why God would allow our child to suffer, while people who intentionally disregarded their own child's safety during pregnancy gave birth to completely healthy children.

What I grew to realize rather quickly after becoming a mother, was that life wasn't fair. Of course, I had learned this tough lesson in other situations during my twenty-seven years on earth and had seen circumstances in other people's lives that proved this point as well. But here lying in front of me was the most tangible proof to-date. The injustice we were facing was based on his comparison to other children and our comparison to other parents. No truer words have ever been spoken than those of Theodore Roosevelt when he said, "Comparison is the thief of joy."

We had been cheated out of the "normal" parenting experience and the happiness that is supposed to accompany one of the greatest moments of our lives. Our child had been cheated out of a life without medical procedures and pain. We felt alone and helpless because no one truly understood what we were going through. Guilt and anger were weighing us down and distracting us from truly relishing our new baby. Joy could not exist where we allowed our attitudes of self-condemnation and bitterness to reside.

The blame game we were playing didn't change who Coleman was or what challenges he was going to face. His issues may or may not have been caused by some faulty gene that one of us carried, chemicals we were exposed to, or medication that we had taken. We may never definitively know the reason why, but dwelling on the past wouldn't make our present any more fulfilling.

My thoughts had to be shifted from the what-ifs, might-have-beens, and should-bes to the current reality we were facing as a family. He was not a mistake but a miracle. He was fearfully and wonderfully created by God for His specific purpose. By focusing on the reason why he was not healthy, I minimized his worth and failed to see his full value in the world, the value that our Heavenly Father gave him. The process of moving past self-blame and anger may seem like an easy one in theory, but really, it was one of the hardest things my freshly broken heart had ever had to do.

> **"For you formed my inward parts; you knitted me together in my mother's womb. I praise you, for I am fearfully and wonderfully made. Wonderful are your works; my soul knows it very well."**
> *Psalm 139:13-14 (ESV)*

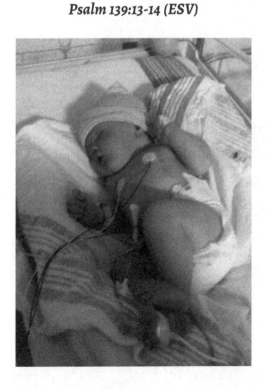

Personal Reflections

Have you ever had experiences where grief and/or anger consumed you and dictated how you responded to your situation? What proof of God's grace is evident now, even if you couldn't see it amid difficulties?

CHAPTER 3

Perfection Redefined

"Coleman, you are a unique and extraordinary little boy. A miraculous mystery that science has yet to figure out. You are writing your own story and refuse to conform to society's standard of normal. Where the doctors see an anomaly, we see perfection. I refuse to let them define you or your worth. You are more than a case study or an article in a medical journal. You are more than a statistic or a predetermined outcome. You are more. You are worthy. You are and will become great things in God's kingdom. We don't fully understand but He does and that gives me peace. You have changed me for the better just by being born, and for that I am thankful every single second of my life."

MRI. CT SCAN. ULTRASOUND. X-ray. EKG. EEG. Every day, another test. Every day, another diagnosis. Each one a single ingredient that would be blended into the recipe of who Coleman would become. The prognosis of every individual diagnosis was a spectrum ranging from mild to severe but layering and intertwining them all into one complex-being diluted the outcomes even further.

The scan of the brain indicated that he was missing his corpus callosum, the band of fibers that connects the hemispheres and allows the left and right side to communicate. He also had a Dandy-Walker Variant, which meant his cerebellum was not formed properly. Documentation of a child having both these conditions was almost nonexistent in medical literature at the time, and his doctors had never seen it in their combined years of experience.

The EKG and ultrasound of his heart revealed three small holes, a patent foramen ovale (PFO), atrial septal defect (ASD), and patent ductus arteriosus (PDA). The cardiologist said that the size and types of defects that he had were not of great concern, and most of them should close-up on their own over time without intervention. The words were reassuring, but the fact remained that his heart had holes in it. Holes that weren't welcomed there.

The rest of the inspection of his inward workings mostly proved to be uneventful. His organs seemed to be close to the correct size, in the correct location, and working up to manufacturer's specs. Thankfully, nothing seemed to be life-threatening or create any urgent concern.

Working from the inside out, the attention then turned to his physical appearance. While skimming his chart for details and trying to see if any new evidence had surfaced between visits from specialists, my eyes hovered over the words "dysmorphic features." Upon further internet research, I learned that this term meant that he had deformed or abnormally shaped physical features. My mind flashed back to my initial conversation with the pediatrician hours after his birth when she had mentioned physical abnormalities. Those words didn't absorb into my consciousness but were lost in the flood of emotions, swirling around without meaning. Now, their menacing connotation caused hesitation and shock.

This tiny person that Mike and I helped create and grow, God purposefully piecing him together with traits of our personalities and looks as well as adding those unique only to him. The beautiful and perfect child that I held in my arms while I softly stroked his hair was being described by terms that detracted from the truth that I saw before me. Hypertelorism. Short philtrum. Webbed neck. Incomplete syndactyly of toes. Hypospadias. Low set ears. A list of foreign vocabulary, all stipulating the strangeness of my son's outward form.

As I intently studied Coleman, soaking in the traits that were deemed medically abnormal, my focus zeroed in on his hands. Oh, his precious little hands were the most distinctive attribute he possessed. His finger joints were oddly placed with his fingers differing in length and all ending with abnormally large finger pads. His thumbs were low set and about the same size as his pinky fingers, which were significantly smaller than average and curved inward. They were constantly balled up into awkward distorted fists, and he would instinctively jerk them away if you tried to touch them. When a doctor pried open his hands in search of a syndrome-verifying singular palmer crease, the blood-curdling screams he released proved that pain was coursing and raging throughout them. I didn't know if I would ever be able to hold those hands or show them how to write his name, but I loved them as I did every other "flawed" part of him.

One morning, as I was attempting to rest in my hospital room, Mike decided to walk to the NICU for a visit. If Mike vanished at any point without explanation, I knew exactly where I could locate him. Snuggled with his boy in the rocking chair next to Coleman's bed solving the world's problems. I never asked what they talked about during their time together, as I felt it wasn't my place to intrude. Sometimes fathers and sons need memories to stay just between them.

As Mike approached, there was a short, slender man standing there staring at our baby. Mike immediately became defensive as the man wasn't dressed in a white coat or scrubs, and his purpose for tampering with our son was unknown. After Mike engaged the stranger in what I can only imagine was a very pleasant, non-confrontational tone, the man informed Mike that he was the new neonatologist that had been assigned to Coleman's case. He was currently off-duty due to the Mardi Gras holiday, hence the street clothes, but was so intrigued by Coleman that he wanted to examine him as soon as possible.

Like most places of business, gossip tends to run rampant through the ranks of hospital employees. The judgements of others spread like wildfire with little bits of manipulated facts being added along the way. Before we were even aware of it, we were being force-fed with opinions of the new neonatologist. Word on the NICU streets was that he had a terrible bedside manner but was in fact, one of the best in his field.

His bland personality and blunt way of disseminating information fed into our belief that he was uncaring and cold-hearted. Because the closest geneticist to our town was two hours away, he scheduled a video chat to brainstorm syndromes and hopefully expedite identifying a genetic cause.

The privacy curtains were drawn, and the other parents were curtly told to cut their visits short so our conference call could commence without interruption. As guilty as I felt for being the reason other parents didn't get to spend precious time with their critically ill babies, I was also selfishly anticipating hearing what the geneticist had to say. As the call was connected and the face of the geneticist appeared on the screen, I instantly placed all my hopes of getting answers on this man's shoulders. He was completely unaware, of course, of the significant amount of pressure he was now under, but I felt it was a great possibility we would have a formal genetic diagnosis by the time Coleman was discharged from the hospital.

My voice was robotic as I spit out the answers to the same questions we had been asked hundreds of times before. Almost trance-like, present in body but far away in the depths of my mind, I sat there as the discussion of unintelligible conditions continued. I was finally snapped back to the real world when the neonatologist quickly stood up and positioned Coleman in his arms, making sure that he was visible on the screen. He held him up close to the camera and twisted him around at various angles so the geneticist could see every anomaly that had been noted. It felt like we were suddenly cast members of *The Greatest Showman*, and our little boy was the next biggest act. I wanted to scream at the top of my lungs that he deserved some dignity and respect because he was a human being and not some science experiment or freak-of-nature, but the words just sat in my throat, unspoken until I could swallow them back down.

As the days passed by, the moment I had been dreading but knew was inevitable had finally arrived. I would be discharged while my child was still admitted in the hospital. Knowing that rushing to my baby's bedside if his condition worsened was now impossible, my palms became sweaty, my chest tightened up, and I became lightheaded at the mere thought of this separation.

We lived about thirty minutes from the hospital when there was no traffic and the weather was perfect. About forty-five if conditions weren't ideal. And about an hour if there was a wreck or road hazard that shut down the main roads and we had to take a detour. Too many obstacles and variables that would delay us in case of an emergency.

The bonding opportunities that experts say are so crucial early on in a child's development are lost forever, but not because you aren't longing to be there every minute of every day. How do those parents do it when their premature or chronically ill children are hospitalized for months and months at a time, but they aren't allowed to stay with them? The strength and courage it must take to walk out of the hospital with empty arms, leaving your entire world at the mercy of the doctors and nurses charged with their care.

When the angel of a social worker we had met with previously came by to check on us, I shared my concerns about being discharged. She explained the undeniable fact that at some point, we would eventually have to return to our house with or without Coleman. She reassured me once again and told me that a break from the hospital might be what I needed to reset my mind and body.

A few hours later, the social worker surprised us again with some good news. One of the transition rooms, where families "room in" with their babies before they are discharged to make sure they are comfortable with the child's care, was available, and we would be allowed to stay there until another family needed it. Instead of going home, we would be literally staying in the NICU only a few feet away from Coleman's pod.

Throughout his hospital stay, we met some incredible nurses as well as some forgettable ones. One of our favorites would always greet us with encouragement and a positive attitude. You could tell that she had a natural gift of caring for the most vulnerable babies in addition to their helpless parents. On one of her night shifts, she pulled us aside and discreetly mentioned that we should ask the neonatologist about his son. The same neonatologist that was emotionally detached from his patients and wasn't a fan of small talk. My shocked expression communicated the skepticism I felt, but she repeated her words followed by "trust me."

The next day, as the neonatologist made his rounds, we waited patiently, bravely ready to ask "the question." The doctor briefly looked over Coleman and informed us that there was no new information that could be shared about his condition. As he went to turn around and walk away, I nervously blurted out, "Would you please share with us about your son?"

He stopped dead in his tracks, his face expressionless and unreadable. My heart beat faster as I was expecting an angry dismissal and started preparing myself for the consequences of my curiosity. Suddenly, he reached up and closed all the curtains so we could have privacy. He said in a hushed tone, "I don't normally talk about my personal life with my patients' families, but since you asked, I want to show you something."

He pulled out his cell phone and began looking through pictures. After a minute or two of searching, he had found the hidden treasure he was seeking and held it up for us to see. His face broke out in a never-before-seen smile as he beamed with pride, "This is my son."

The individual in the picture looked to be around my age and seemed full of joy as he sat on the back of a uniquely made bicycle. Physically, he was a grown man but developmentally, he was only on a four-year old level. He had developed typically for the first few years of his life but then one day, he stopped. No explanation or diagnosis explaining why. The neonatologist said as a medical professional, he wanted science to explain what had happened and used his position in the community to try to get answers. He and his wife were frustrated and heartbroken over their son's situation with no hope in sight.

He and his wife had to make a choice. Either meet their child where he was and do everything in their power to make his life fulfilling and rewarding or stay weighed down by their despair and what should have been. They chose to embrace their child fully.

The doctor said that his son loved to ride bicycles but didn't have the motor skills to ride independently or the strength to ride on the back of a typical two-person bike. Instead of accepting defeat, he found an adaptive bike that could meet his son's needs by hooking onto the back of a regular bicycle. Their biking excursions didn't fit the typical mold, but by thinking outside of the box, they were able to create memories and experiences that added quality to their lives.

While Mike and I had been mourning the life we would never have and the disappointments we were facing because of Coleman's challenges, the doctor's story was like a glimmer of sunshine on a stormy day. We graciously thanked the doctor for showing us that happiness was possible again, and the only barrier to that happiness would be ones that we created ourselves. Our heartbreak didn't miraculously dissipate after that conversation, but it gave us hope that things would get better. They had to get better.

God uses people at certain times in our lives to speak truth into us when we are so consumed by our own suffering that we are unable to see the good that can come from it. We were not the only parents to have a child with a disability, a rare disorder, an unknown future. We were not the only parents facing grief and heartbreak, wishing things were different. We were not alone. There was some unexplainable peace that came with knowing that others had walked in the shoes we were currently wearing and felt the pain that we were currently feeling.

Not long after our encounter with the neonatologist, a friend shared with us the poem, "Welcome to Holland" by Emily Perl Kingsley (1). Although it had been well circulated for many years, I had not had the opportunity to read it until this divinely appointed moment in time. It so perfectly articulated what I was feeling and experiencing that I broke down in snotty, screeching sobs. Our family had just landed in Holland.

> **"Rejoice in hope, be patient in tribulation, be constant in prayer."**
> **Romans 12:12 (ESV)**

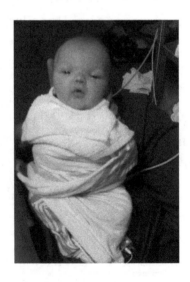

AN EXCEPTIONAL LIFE

Welcome To Holland
by Emily Perl Kingsley

I am often asked to describe the experience of raising a child with a disability - to try to help people who have not shared that unique experience to understand it, to imagine how it would feel. It's like this......

When you're going to have a baby, it's like planning a fabulous vacation trip - to Italy. You buy a bunch of guide books and make your wonderful plans. The Coliseum. The Michelangelo David. The gondolas in Venice. You may learn some handy phrases in Italian. It's all very exciting.

After months of eager anticipation, the day finally arrives. You pack your bags and off you go. Several hours later, the plane lands. The flight attendant comes in and says, "Welcome to Holland."

"Holland?!?" you say. "What do you mean Holland?? I signed up for Italy! I'm supposed to be in Italy. All my life I've dreamed of going to Italy."

But there's been a change in the flight plan. They've landed in Holland and there you must stay.

The important thing is that they haven't taken you to a horrible, disgusting, filthy place, full of pestilence, famine and disease. It's just a different place.

So you must go out and buy new guide books. And you must learn a whole new language. And you will meet a whole new group of people you would never have met.

It's just a different place. It›s slower-paced than Italy, less flashy than Italy. But after you›ve been there for a while and you catch your breath, you look around.... and you begin to notice that Holland has windmills....and Holland has tulips. Holland even has Rembrandts.

But everyone you know is busy coming and going from Italy... and they're all bragging about what a wonderful time they had there. And for the rest of your life, you will say "Yes, that's where I was supposed to go. That's what I had planned."

And the pain of that will never, ever, ever, ever go away... because the loss of that dream is a very very significant loss.

But... if you spend your life mourning the fact that you didn't get to Italy, you may never be free to enjoy the very special, the very lovely things ... about Holland.

Personal Reflections

Reflect on a time in your life when you felt hopeless. How were you able to find joy and focus on the hope in Christ Jesus instead of your current circumstances? Have you ever let gossip dictate your opinion of someone, and what were the consequences of doing so?

CHAPTER 4

The Sound of Silence

"All of the words of comfort and the 'I love yous' that were said but not heard come rushing back to me. Those moments when you were crying and had your eyes closed. Those moments when I was out of your sight or out of reach to calm you with my touch. Did you feel alone and scared? Did you think we weren't there for you? I am so sorry that I didn't know how to communicate with you during those first days of your life. Never again, sweet boy. We will give you a voice, whether spoken or signed. A way that you can communicate and tell us what you want and need. You will never be isolated because we didn't do our part as parents. We will give you everything required for you to experience life to the fullest, however hard it may be, because a small bit of effort is nothing compared to what you deserve."

SMELLING THE AROMA OF freshly baked cookies wafting through the kitchen. Feeling a cool breeze blowing through your hair on a brisk fall day. Tasting freshly brewed coffee as it awakens you early in the morning. Hearing a much anticipated "I love you" from someone close to your heart. Witnessing your firstborn walk down the aisle on her wedding day.

Our five senses allow us to consume, digest, and interpret our daily experiences. Without realizing it, our bodies capture samples from our environment, sending the information to our brain for processing. Our brain then formulates an appropriate response for us to engage and interact with our surroundings. It is an intricate choreographed movement of impulses on the tangled web of nerves traveling to and from the body's operating hub. Because most people are born with the ability to use all five of their senses effortlessly, we tend to take for granted the possibility that one or more of those senses could be dulled or lost completely.

As Coleman got stronger and continued to grow, we knew his stay in the NICU would soon be coming to an end. We had gotten the boot from the transition room we had been allowed to stay in for a few nights because another family was ready to begin the discharge process. With brave faces on, Mike and I headed home for the first time in nine days. As scared as I was to leave without my baby, a break from the hospital setting was a refreshing and much needed change of scenery. Fresh off a semi-decent night's sleep, armed with the night's supply of breast milk, we headed back to the hospital.

As mandated by state law (2), every newborn in Louisiana is given a hearing test before being discharged from the hospital or birthing facility. The NICU nurse-on-duty informed us that the hospital audiologist would be stopping by in a few minutes to perform the testing, and then we would be required to attend a first aid/CPR class as part of the discharge protocol.

The audiologist appeared and began setting up the machine and placing the electrodes on Coleman's head while he lay soundly sleeping, all snuggled up in a hospital-issued blanket. Mike was a master swaddler. The way he wrapped and tucked was awe-inspiring, and Coleman would immediately calm down and fall asleep within seconds. I, on the other hand, was not skilled in the art of swaddling, and he would always get his hands and feet free, which inevitably woke him up. Since the hearing test required the patient to be sleeping, Mike stepped up and quickly handled business.

Explaining that Coleman had failed his previous two otoacoustic emission (OAE) tests, the audiologist informed us that she was now performing an auditory brainstem response (ABR) test to verify hearing loss. Interestingly enough, we were unaware that he had even had previous hearing tests, much less failed them.

I am sure somewhere in the depths of the handwritten notes documenting Coleman's existence, there was something scribbled down recording his failures, but no such evidence had been shared with us, his parents.

Many babies fail their initial tests, we were assured, because fluid or other debris can get stuck in the ear canal during birth. With a confident tone, the audiologist quickly put to rest any fear that he was deaf.

Mike and I were seated at the foot of the crib watching, waiting intently. As the sound stimulus was initiated, softly at first and then working louder each time, he never even flinched. We could hear the loudest tones from our seats several feet away. My heart sank. The audiologist silently made notes, avoiding eye contact. I felt like it was a prank, a practical joke where any minute someone would pop out from behind a wall and tell us that none of it was real. It wasn't really the deafness that was hard to swallow but the deafness plus his cognitive and physical disabilities. Not knowing how we would be able to adapt to, teach, and communicate with Coleman with all his senses intact was arduous enough, but now we would have to effectively accomplish those goals without using his ability to hear.

We were handed generic pamphlets with images of happy, smiling families on the covers followed by the audiologist's heartfelt condolences. He would need a follow-up ABR test in a few weeks to get an official hearing loss diagnosis, which would get him automatically enrolled in early intervention services.

Still reeling from yet another unexpected discovery, off we rushed to our first aid/CPR class. Staring blankly at the instructor and ignoring every word that she said, Mike and I sat numbly in the hard, uncomfortable chairs. My mind drifted back to when I was pregnant. I had read books, sang songs, and talked to him throughout the nine months. I wanted him to recognize his momma's voice and know that it meant comfort and love.

Following popular pregnancy trends, we had placed headphones on my inflated belly and softly played classical music to try to stimulate brain development in utero. Since Coleman didn't react in the slightest to our classical music selections, Mike suggested, playfully, that maybe he was a fan of a different genre of music, one with much more bass. Going along with him, I cranked up a playlist with a mix of hard rock, rap, and blues, and the child started doing cartwheels in my womb.

Hindsight is 20/20 and suddenly everything came into focus. He never heard any of the music we played, he just felt the vibrations. He never heard any of the stories I read or songs I sang. He never heard my voice or how much I loved him. His world was filled with complete silence.

Deafness was the only diagnosis that he had received since birth that we immediately knew the outcome. His hearing loss couldn't get any worse or progress over time. It was also not going to get any better on its own. Finally, something was known and definitive. We only had one answer among the millions of questions, but it allowed us an ounce of control in an otherwise unmanageable situation.

One of Mike's top ten, all-time favorite movies is *Mr. Holland's Opus*. I have come home so many times over the course of our marriage to find him shamelessly sobbing on the couch while watching music teacher/composer, Mr. Holland, finally step up to be the father he needed to be for his deaf son. Like the Hollands, music is very important to our family. Every aspect of our lives has a theme song, and music is continuously playing in our home.

We had selfishly hoped to pass our love for music down to our son, who coincidentally shares the same nickname as the deaf character in the movie. Like Mike said shortly after we received the news, how do you explain a song like "Wild Horses" from The Rolling Stones to someone who has never heard it? It was impossible and devastating.

Towards the end of the movie, there is a scene where Mr. Holland finally accepts that his son is deaf and invests his time to learn and perform "Beautiful Boy" by John Lennon in sign language at a school concert. His child, whom he had previously been unable to communicate with or relate to, is now a grown man. So much time had passed, but at the climax of the movie, their relationship is mended. Not because Mr. Holland was an excellent signer or would be the perfect parent from that point on. It was because of the effort that he finally put forth. The effort translated to love. A soul-shaking, heart-wrenching epiphany.

Later that evening, we were moved into a transition room, and our sweet Coleman got to come with us. We weren't squatters this go-round, but had become official residents, at least for the required two-night-stay. No monitors or nurses present to make sure everything was going well, but if something did go wrong, a quick medical response was just a button push away. The uneasiness of why the doctors suddenly determined that he was healthy enough to be discharged hung over my head like a dark cloud. Although stable, his condition had not changed, and we still didn't have any answers as to what had caused all his anomalies and health issues. Just hours before, his heart and oxygen rate were being monitored constantly, but now, no one seemed concerned.

All we had to do was keep him alive that first night, a practice run to determine if we could be trusted with the care of our son. If we could do it one night, then we could probably do it two. After two, we would receive our "Outstanding Parents" award and be allowed to take him home.

It was a glorious and exhausting victory to hear his cry every two hours when his tummy would become empty, and he was ready for a snack. We were still not having success with breastfeeding, so I continued pumping and bottle feeding him at the same time. He was a ferocious eater and would devour the entire bottle every time. Our little fighter was bulking up for battle.

The morning after our second and final night in the transition room, the nurse came in with the discharge packet. She quickly reviewed all the information, including several follow-up appointments that had already been scheduled with various specialists. Like holding my head under a waterfall with my mouth agape, I tried drinking in the flood of information raining down on me, hoping to swallow at least a few drops. My awareness impaired by lack of sleep and exhaustion, I nodded in understanding while trying to hide the look of confusion on my face. Fake it 'til you make it, and making it was our only option.

As we packed up our bags, preparing for our voyage home, we snapped the obligatory photographs that most new parents cherish from this historic event. Our photographs were unlike the typical: a heaviness displayed in each frame reflecting, with glaring honesty, Coleman's differences.

He wasn't dressed in his expensive designer outfit that we had meticulously selected for this occasion because I couldn't remember where I had placed it in the confusion of the previous thirteen days. Holding him in one arm and talking on my cell phone with the other, I wasn't calling people with excitement to tell them we were being discharged. I was on the phone with a doctor's office scheduling yet another appointment for my newborn baby.

Our smiles in the photographs were a façade, successfully masking the fear and insecurities that hid underneath. What was supposed to be such a happy, joyous celebration turned into one that was riddled with trauma and lost opportunities. Every time the lullaby would play over the hospital loudspeaker indicating a new baby had been born, the pang of jealousy and bitterness that I had successfully put aside earlier, overwhelmed me once again. A passing whiff of the soap we had used to wash our hands before visiting him in the NICU would trigger an onslaught of anxiety and unpleasant feelings for months or even years after he was discharged.

When I least expect it, those same emotions will still sucker punch me, leaving me doubled over in pain, gasping for air. Being an only child, it is easy to forget how delayed Coleman is compared to his peers. But reality checks are all around us. A social media posting of someone's child who is the same age or younger accomplishing milestones that he is nowhere near being able to meet. Desperately, wanting "normal" holiday experiences as a family, but he isn't interested in gifts or the festivities. Receiving invitations to birthday parties and witnessing his inability to appropriately play with peers. These situations are the worst. The absolute worst. I am very skilled at holding in the tears until I can get to the privacy of my car or house, but sometimes the tears decide to fall with force. Friends try to comfort me and, although sincere and filled with love, their words lack true empathy because how could they really know.

I throw my pity party, a grand event with an exclusive guest list. Streamers are hung from the ceiling, balloons are filled with helium, amazing center pieces are placed along the tabletops, and of course, there is a cake. The cake is usually real because I also like to eat my feelings during times such as these. Once all the fun has been had, I make sure the party ends at a reasonable hour, clean up the mess, and call it a night.

Although these moments are cruel and extremely painful, I have become stronger and more resilient each time I face them. God is growing and shaping me spiritually and emotionally to face whatever tomorrow may bring. The sadness and hurt is temporary, not to be dwelled on or wallowed in for extended periods of time. Sorting through muddled emotions, consciously deciding to accept the current circumstances of our lives with Coleman and avoiding an attitude of negativity is an on-going struggle that began in the NICU and will continue until I take my last breath on earth.

Denial and indifference would only hinder my attempts to supply him with the love and support he needed to thrive. Setting up camp and settling in a place of pity and regret would prevent me from fully embracing the blessings that God had graciously provided. I wanted to become Mr. Holland at the end of the movie, standing on the stage, meeting my son right where he was instead of wishing he were somewhere else. I wouldn't be waiting twenty years to act intentionally with love but would be doing so at the beginning of Coleman's life instead.

Deaf or hearing. Cognitively delayed or intellectually gifted. Non-mobile or an Olympic athlete. One extreme or the other. Anywhere in between. Coleman would need us to try. Try to figure out his needs. Try to adapt things in our daily lives to help him achieve goals. Try to teach the world how to include someone so amazing. By us trying, even if we weren't successful, we were showing him how much we truly loved him. And that was the most important motivation of all.

> **"Count it all joy, my brothers, when you meet trials of various kinds, for you know that the testing of your faith produces steadfastness."**
> **James 1:2-3 (ESV)**

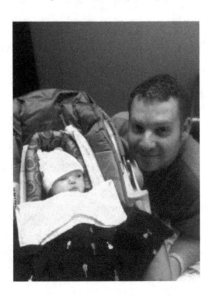

Personal Reflections

Name some major disappointments that you have experienced in your life. How did you react when life didn't go as planned? Was spiritual growth and maturity a result of experiencing those trials?

CHAPTER 5

Home Bittersweet Home

"Even though we won't be at your side every moment of every day, we will be your protectors and defenders. We will try to make the best decisions, so that you will have the highest quality of life and get the same opportunities that every other child gets to experience. I wish that I already knew the outcome. What our lives will look like in five, ten, or twenty years. If I just knew, I could prepare for whatever is in store for us. I would be able to face the good, bad, joyous, and heartbreaking with the confidence in knowing how it all turns out in the end. But that isn't how any of this works. My fears of being surprised by yet another diagnosis or condition cannot be put to rest because there is no magic ball to see the future. I must trust that God will help us through whatever storms we face in the future as He has faithfully done up to this point. That is the promise that will carry us through."

SECURELY FASTENED INTO HIS car seat, Coleman began his trek home from the hospital. The world around us seemed to be moving in fast motion, speeding by with complete disregard to the precious cargo we were transporting. Like explorers in uncharted wilderness, we slowly drove forward, anticipating every danger and preparing for unknown ambushes. We were on our own and responsible for this helpless human being's safety and survival.

Blinkers were put on a quarter mile before turns. Speed limits were not even close to being exceeded. A safety cushion was provided on all sides of the vehicle to account for, just in case, another drivers' complete incompetence. I sat in the backseat next to Coleman while Mike drove, so that I could provide for his every need before he even realized he needed it. It was the longest, most terrifying road trip of our lives.

When we arrived home late that afternoon, and carefully carried him and our belongings inside the house, there was finally a sense of normalcy. We were on a level playing field with every other new parent for the first time since he was born. Mike worked his swaddle magic, and we laid him in his crib. He was so tiny and exposed in his enormous crib. So vulnerable.

Our house was relatively small at right under 1,200 square feet. A fixer-upper starter home in a well

-established neighborhood perfect for young families like ours. Nothing fancy but cozy and full of love. The three bedrooms were all positioned down a short hallway, and Coleman's room sat catty-cornered from the master bedroom. His bedding was up to the U.S. Consumer Product Safety Commission's standards, and we had installed a video monitor aimed directly at him. If he was in distress, I could reach him in exactly five running steps from our bed (I have long legs).

As close as his bed was to ours, it still wasn't close enough. I needed him within arms-reach so I could feel his existence and warmth during the night. I needed to hear his breath knowing that life was still present and had not snuck away while my consciousness had drifted into deep slumbers. The fear was that I would relax and unknowingly allow something tragic to occur only to find out in the morning when it was too late. Too late to resuscitate and save my Coleman.

As a baby shower gift, we had received a portable crib that included an accessory to convert it to a bassinet for newborns. It would fit perfectly at the foot of our bed and would allow immediate access to him for feedings or unforeseen emergencies. We dragged that thing out of its bag and began trying to put it together. Both Mike and I have college degrees and are of average intelligence. Mike is also very mechanically minded. Putting together a portable crib should be no big deal for the two of us, right? Wrong. So very wrong. We would set it up ... and it would collapse in on itself. Every try ended with the same result. Words were exchanged and our marriage tested, but finally, something clicked. Not in our minds like a light bulb moment but on the actual crib. It had finally locked into place and was ready to become the baby's bed.

That first night at home went as well as could be expected. He would awaken and cry around every two hours to be fed. Since he still was unable to latch, I continued to bottle feed him while I pumped. There was no need to wake Mike since I had to be awake anyway to pump, but he would usually sit up with me pretending not to be exhausted so I wouldn't feel alone.

After his discharge from the NICU, we were told to monitor and track Coleman's body temperature and output to ensure he was regulating his body processes properly. All newborns have difficulty with temperature regulation initially, but eventually, they can do so naturally.

At some point during the first night, Coleman's hands and feet had escaped the cocoon I had wrapped him in, and he became chilled. He woke us up, crying in a tone that was unfamiliar to me. One of discomfort and not hunger. I checked his temperature, and it was very low. The low reading must have been because I hadn't placed the thermometer correctly under his arm. I kept checking his temperature, and it continued to register very low. As he screamed and wiggled in his uncomfortable state, I started panicking and hysterically telling Mike that he was too cold. Mike calmly replied, "Wrap him back up in blankets. Telling me repeatedly that he is cold isn't going to make him any warmer." He made complete sense, and I admitted that I may have overreacted a small bit. Night one of independent parenting . . . nailed it.

The week before Coleman was born, Mike had accepted a new job with great benefits. We had planned it all out where he would be able to stay home with us for a week before having to leave for a two-week training in Dallas, Texas. That was the plan if Coleman had been born healthy and had gotten discharged two days after birth, which obviously did not happen. Thankfully, Mike's new company was very understanding and accommodating. They told him to take all the time he needed for his family, but it had been almost three weeks so we knew he would have to leave soon.

Our families both lived out of town but were within a three-hour commute of us. My mom still worked but offered to use her vacation time to come stay with Coleman and me during the first week of Mike's training. I was deeply relieved because other than Mike, my parents are the only people in the world that truly understand my anxiety and how to deal with me during those darkest times. I had done fairly well since we had gotten home but mainly because I was too exhausted to be anxious. Exhaustion was definitely a blessing during those first few days.

As Mike departed to embark on his new job opportunity, my mom arrived to fill in on baby duty. I still had someone to hold him while I showered and wash bottles while I napped. Although I was too tired the first night at home to figure out that I needed to wrap my cold baby in a blanket, I wasn't too tired to calculate Mike and my salaries to figure out if we could afford to hire a nanny to stay with us full time. Maybe it was because the numbers were so low and the math was very easy to calculate, but I figured out rather quickly that the answer was no. Our lower-middle class existence would have to continue without hired help.

My mom's stay seemed to end in a blink of an eye, and soon I was going solo. In addition to me trying to keep the child alive, fed, and changed alone, my emotional support person would be leaving me for the second time in two weeks. I was still not taking any anxiety medication because I was feeding Coleman breastmilk and didn't want to take any chances of him having side effects. Basically, my anxiety had anxiety. My thoughts were consumed with how all my safety nets and coping mechanisms were not working. If my life during this time had a theme, anxiety would be it.

As redundant as the topic may seem throughout our story, it was intertwined into every second of my day. Physically, I was worn down from the constant mental attack and fighting to try to cope and function. Even when it would let up for a period of time, it would never completely disappear and would eventually rear its ugly head to hit me harder than it had before. If you have never experienced it, words aren't adequate to describe the feeling. Imagine being trapped in a small box against your will with no way out. Claustrophobic, screaming for help, feeling your chest tighten and not being able to catch your breath with no relief in sight. There wasn't a single trigger, but anything could make me spiral out of control.

I wasn't depressed and never had thoughts of harming myself or Coleman, but I couldn't give him all the attention he needed because my mind was so distracted. Once again, I was feeling robbed of experiencing that ideal parenting scenario we had read about in books. The unfairness and cruelty of it all slowly crept back in.

The night before Mike was to return from training, I started feeling ill and had a terrible migraine. I had not had a migraine since I was a kid, but this one seemed to make up for lost time. I would get nauseous if I tried to move and lights caused excruciating pain. I gathered the baby and his supplies and parked myself in the recliner with him for the night. Our dog was extremely concerned about me as well and even laid on my legs as if to say, "I'm here to help you, momma." I was in too much pain to go to sleep but would close my eyes and cry in between Cole's feedings. As my fever rose, the chills became more violent until I was almost convulsing. I noticed some pain in one of my breasts when I was pumping but it wasn't anything terrible. Since I had the lights off, I assumed it was just normal breast-feeding discomfort.

The next morning when the sun rose, I finally saw that my breast was blood red, extremely painful, and twice its original size. Although the instant augmentation had taken me by surprise, I quickly realized the reason for the increase in size and other symptoms was actually mastitis.

I called my general practitioner's office as soon as they opened and declared the urgency of me needing to be seen immediately. My ob-gyn's office was about thirty minutes away, and I knew I couldn't drive there feeling so ill, so I decided this was the best option. This should have been the point that I called someone to watch the baby while someone else drove me to the doctor. Honestly, that option never crossed my mind. A little bit panicky, I loaded him up in the car and drove myself to the doctor's office five minutes away.

Upon entering the waiting room carrying my one-month old son, I was quickly taken back to an exam room and assessed by the nurse. Since my GP didn't have any openings that morning, his nurse practitioner came in soon after to see me. When she looked at my engorged, infected breast, her first response was, "Oh, my goodness," quickly followed by, "I will be right back." She ran out of the room and returned less than a minute later with the doctor.

The doctor said that it was a miracle it hadn't abscessed and caused me to become septic, but he thought we had caught it in time. He gave me a massive dose of antibiotics in a shot and prescribed me oral antibiotics. He told me to go straight to the emergency room if any of my symptoms worsened or I continued to run fever. While I was waiting on my shot, Mike rushed into the exam room. The look on his face was one of relief and deep concern. He was relieved to finally be home with his little family, but the doctor's report had confirmed that his worry was completely justified.

After a few days, I recovered fully but my breast milk supply didn't. Pouring out those hard-earned drops of tainted milk was almost as painful as the infection itself. A couple of weeks later, I had a relapse of mastitis but in the other breast. It wasn't as severe but basically ended my ability to pump. We began his transition to formula at around six weeks old. As sad as I was to have to quit breastfeeding, it was also a relief because he started sleeping through the night. As my return to working full-time was quickly approaching, I was thankful for all the rest I could get.

Utilizing my creative-thinking skills, I dreamt up the idea that if I could stockpile sleep, I would have enough energy to push me through going back to work, caring for an infant with special needs, and being a single mother while my husband was away at work. This little fantasy world I created with unicorns and rainbows somehow led me to believe that the transition would be manageable, if not easy. I mean, other moms and dads did it all the time, and so could I. Cue the superhero costume and lack of self-care.

I have always longed to be a stay-at-home mother but, not knowing what the future held, Mike and I both felt that I needed to work while I was still able. Coleman's health might deteriorate, or his care become more complicated, so we wanted to be financially prepared. We had applied for Social Security Disability Insurance and Medicaid but were told that we made too much money to qualify for assistance. Since the approval is based on income and family size, even if one of us had quit our jobs, we still wouldn't qualify.

The frustration and feelings of injustice mounted. Our child with multiple diagnoses that automatically classified him as disabled was denied financial assistance because we worked and didn't have multiple children. The process didn't take into consideration the amount of medical bills that we paid out of pocket, but solely focused on the amount of money we were bringing in. This was our first of many experiences that showed us how truly unfair the system is for families like ours.

Mike had come in from work one night having picked up some fast food for dinner. I grabbed the mail to sort through as we sat around the table to eat. A few pieces of junk mail. Some sales papers from local grocery stores with great prices on ground meat. And a letter from the hospital where Coleman was born. I tore into the letter expecting it to be a bill of some sort, but what I saw caused me to burst into tears. It was undeniably a bill, that part I got correct. Instead of it being the amount that I had learned was our deductible or out-of-pocket maximum, it was for the grand total of $187,000.

The bill was more than what our house was worth. How would we ever be able to afford to pay this off? The desperation led me to wonder how much a semi-healthy kidney would go for on the black market. I mean, I do have two of them so that would be the organ of choice if it got to that point. After the hyperventilating ceased and I regained a little bit of my composure, I went and placed my dinner in the refrigerator to consume at a later time, when my appetite had returned.

Early the next morning, my time was spent staring at the clock and waiting for it to turn to eight, which was when the business office at the hospital opened. I practiced and rehearsed what I was going to say, trying to sound desperate but not too emotional. I normally try to avoid difficult conversations in general, especially ones conducted over the phone, so this situation caused a large amount of stress.

Hands shaking, I pressed send. The person that answered on the other end, read her script in a monotone voice, basically uninterested in anything but being left alone. I calmly explained our situation and asked if there could possibly be some mistake with our account. As I was placed on hold for what felt like an eternity, I knew she would return to tell me there was indeed a mistake with the account. Instead of owing $187,000, we really owed $287,000. Luckily, when she picked back up, she informed me that the charges had not yet been sent to the insurance companies for approval prior to the bill being sent out. She verified the policy information and said to disregard the bill for the time being.

We would be getting an explanation of benefits from the two insurance companies after they processed the claims, then we would receive an updated bill for the remaining balance from the hospital. The updated bill turned out to be a much more manageable amount, and I was thankfully able to keep all my critical organs.

Similar conversations with hospitals, doctors' offices, and insurance companies about various issues would become a normal part of my life. Something that I would grow to be very comfortable doing. I was learning to be assertive, confident, and an advocate, all skills that I didn't possess naturally but that would be necessary to fight for my child. Strapping on those boxing gloves, I would fight Coleman's fight. Yelling at the top of my lungs, I would be his voice. Even if I got knocked down or silenced, I would never, never quit.

"Open your mouth for the mute, for the rights of all who are destitute. Open your mouth, judge righteously, defend the rights of the poor and needy."
Proverbs 31:8-9 (ESV)

Personal Reflections

Have you ever had to be someone's voice and advocate for them because they couldn't do so themselves? How is Christ the ultimate advocate? Who is our helper mentioned in John 15:26? When have you had to face your fears head-on and what was the outcome? List scriptures that help you cope when faced with injustice or unfairness.

CHAPTER 6

Amended Expectations

"Take your time, sweet Coleman, we will meet you where you are. Time goes by so quickly and children grow up so fast, but you are doing your own thing. You are writing your own book one chapter at a time. It is so easy to want to rush life along, but we are getting to hang on to moments that usually vanish in the blink of an eye. Until you are ready and able, we will wait. Our expectations of how your story will go will never diminish the pride we will feel as we turn each page, uncovering the endless surprises and plot twists you have in store for us. We love you just as you are, as God created you to be."

SIX WEEKS. THE LENGTH of time that I got to spend with my newborn before having to go back to work full time. Of those six weeks, he was hospitalized for two of them. I had spent less time with my baby than most mother dogs spend with their puppies before they can be separated to find new homes. If puppies are removed any sooner, it is considered inhumane, but no one batted an eye at me having to leave my offspring in the care of others at a month and a half old. It is a normal, accepted practice in the world of working parents.

Prior to giving birth, I had arranged for a good friend to keep Coleman when the time came for me to venture back into the workforce. She operated an in-home daycare that was located about ten minutes from my office. Since Coleman didn't have a trach or feeding tube, his care at this point was that of a typical six-week old baby. He just needed to be fed, changed, and loved. Although I was dreading having to go back to work and leaving him, I needed to return for financial security and insurance benefits.

The first day back to work was very emotional. I held in my tears on the commute to the sitter's house, but as I pulled into her driveway at 7:00 a.m., I wasn't sure I would be able to go through with it. Dropping off my most prized possession and entrusting someone else with his care was much more difficult than I had ever imagined. Giving over control of Coleman's well-being and believing he would be loved and cared for in the same way as he would be at home with me was pushing the limits of my sanity. It took every bit of my self-control to not turn the car around and head back to the comfort of our house.

The industry I work in is male-dominated, and I am the only female at our location. I knew I would have to put on a brave face and pretend that I wasn't wrecked inside as I walked through the office door. I didn't want to be that overly emotional female who made everyone else uncomfortable, not for their sake but for my own. I wanted to prove that I was okay and unbreakable.

Since most of my coworkers had children, thinking back on their own personal experiences helped them recognize how hard it must have been for me that day. Although not confirmed, I assume that some of their wives helped remind them to take extra special care of me as well. The group took me to lunch at my favorite restaurant and made me feel that there would be a sense of routine and normalcy again soon. After a few hours and numerous texts from the sitter showing a happy, living baby, I was able to settle into my new role as a working mother.

My employer has always been extremely kind and generous for allowing me to work flexible hours to be able to meet Coleman's medical and therapy needs, which alleviated a lot of undue pressure. Many employers create added stress by prioritizing work over family and are unwilling to make accommodations for their employees. I have heard heartbreaking stories of friends having to choose between providing financially for their family and caring for their child's complex needs, a position no parent should ever be in. Such scenarios greatly contrast my own experience with being a working mom of a special needs child, and it reminds me to be incredibly thankful every single day that I can do both successfully.

During my college career and at different jobs over the years, I have had the opportunity to complete the Myers-Briggs Type Indicator personality test (3) several times. The test was developed by a mother/daughter duo who took a well-established psychological theory of how people perceive their world, relationships, and decision-making and put it into a questionnaire format. The questions reflect a person's personality traits in the following categories: introversion or extraversion, sensing or intuition, thinking, or feeling, judging or perception. Each person has a preference within each category giving a total of sixteen possible results. Within a diverse group of people, the results can help prevent conflict where certain personality differences might otherwise create friction. Outside of the corporate, church or school setting, it can also provide personal insight into why a person behaves a certain way in certain environments.

Every time I took the test, I got the same result: INFJ. My preferences are Introversion (I), Intuition (N), Feeling (F), and Judgement (J). This is the rarest of all personality types, making up less than one percent of the current population, and it describes who I am perfectly. It is known as "The Advocate" personality, which is fitting since I was involuntarily taking on that role for my son. This personality type has some pretty amazing strengths like creativity, altruism, determination/passion, and decisiveness, just to name a few. The weaknesses, however, are where I can relate to the most: sensitive, extremely private, perfectionist, and easily burned out.

I wanted to be perfect. I wanted to have my life together. I wanted to balance work and family and give my all to both. I wanted to be strong and brave. If I wasn't, someone might see the cracks and brokenness underneath the surface. It wasn't something that I intentionally did to deceive people, but it was my survival instinct. Protect yourself from the judging and clueless populations by never letting them see the raw, painful truth of your existence. I so longed to connect with others that understood our circumstances but opening-up and exposing the fact that I was completely overwhelmed was terrifying. Mike and I leaned on each other for support. He was the only one to see my full vulnerability, and I, his. We were never broken at the same time so one of us could always step up and be the comforter.

Being a parent of a child with disabilities is a marathon, not a sprint. As an avid but not naturally talented runner, I am well aware of the differences in training for both type races. You must pace yourself much differently to run 26.2 miles than shorter distances. You must hydrate properly, give yourself time to recover from runs, and keep going whenever you hit "the wall." This event usually occurs around mile twenty, and you literally feel like you have run into a brick wall, hence the term. You feel you don't have the physical or mental energy to take another step toward the finish line. All you want to do is eat a snack, take a nap, and never run again. But you keep pushing, putting one foot in front of the other. You haven't trained all those weeks and months to quit now. Besides, your car is parked miles away and there are no taxi services on the race route. Basically, you have no other option but to keep going.

As you continue forward progress, each step gets a little less daunting. The physical pain is still nearly unbearable, but it is easier than it was ten minutes ago. Finally, you reach the finish line and feel the pride and accomplishment of having overcome the obstacles and discomfort. You are a different person than when you started the race.

Coleman was less than two months old, and I was full steam ahead, sprinting as fast as I could. In addition to returning to work full-time, all Coleman's specialist follow-up appointments had begun. Running on fumes, but our race was just beginning and there was no finish line in sight. I truly don't know how I survived that first year other than by the grace of God. His arms secured under-mine, holding me up when my strength was depleted. He replenished my soul with the peace of His promises, even when physical rest had escaped my reach.

Upon discharge from the hospital, Coleman was automatically enrolled in our state's early intervention program, Early Steps (ES). The first step in receiving services was to have a full evaluation done to figure out which areas of development he was delayed in. At this age, the criteria was vague and subjective but the evaluator noted his significant lack of head support, floppy muscle tone (hypotonia), and deafness. The evaluation results were more than enough to qualify him for services, so our lives got even more hectic.

I would receive multiple phone calls and text messages a week related to early intervention. The calls came from Coleman's caseworker, evaluator, special instructor, teacher of the deaf, physical therapist, and speech therapist. We had to schedule visits, sign paperwork, review progress notes, and get our "homework" to do each day from each of the interventionists. Next, came the calls and requests from the State Office for Citizens with Developmental Disabilities (OCDD) to get Coleman on the seven-year waiting list for Medicaid Waivers. We had to get the documentation of Coleman's delays from the ES case worker and provide them periodically to the OCDD caseworker. To prevent boredom because we had so much free time, we started taking Coleman to a private physical therapist weekly to receive additional assistance with his tone issues. It was an endless coordination of schedules, communication, and documentation.

The instructors and therapists that worked with him were all wonderful. However, some of them had an acute case of tunnel vision, only focusing on their particular area of expertise. Failing to look at the big picture and him as a whole-being, they were unable to realize that there were multiple gears working together to make the wheels turn. The feedback and suggestions they provided only added to my never-ending to-do list, and I spent most of our precious spare time working on skills with Coleman that other children accomplish with little effort. My perfectionist mentality wanted to accomplish everything we were told to work on as "homework" because I didn't want to be chastised and made to feel like we weren't doing enough for our child. Although not intentional, the passion of certain therapists was easily misconstrued as a reprimand, which no parent wants to receive. Many of the suggestions also contradicted what other professionals had told us or the therapists would outright criticize another person's approach to treatment. We were already blindly navigating this unknown world, unsure if we were making the right decisions regarding Coleman's care, and now we had to try to decipher what advice or approach was most credible.

As the stress and overwhelming pressure to know everything and do everything correctly came to a head, God sent me reassurance through our precious miracle. Having just laid Coleman down on his custom sewn changing pad, he looked up at me with his dark brown, almond shaped eyes. Just as I was wondering if he was even aware of his surroundings or of me, the most beautiful smile stretched what seemed like a mile across his tiny little face. It wasn't a gas smile or an involuntary reflex. It was deliberate and beautifully healing.

Life cannot be experienced on a to-do list. It cannot be managed and controlled to the point where the outcome is predetermined. It took many, many months which turned into years, but at some point, I realized that we had to find a balance between expectations and reality. We would do our best to provide Coleman the opportunities he needed to catch up and to make developmental progress but not at the expense of our mental health or our family. Loving him, enjoying him, and making memories as a family were now our priority.

Each decision, whether major or minor, felt like it held the weight of the world and if the wrong one was made, then everything would come crashing down. I didn't want to be held hostage by the feeling of failure. If I couldn't get around to completing my list or if I made the wrong decision about a treatment plan, tomorrow was a new day and I could try again. My amended expectations helped me realize that the world kept turning regardless of failure and that there wasn't a true right or wrong way to accomplish goals. Life is an educated guess and then adapting to whatever circumstances happen next. The feeling of freedom when I gave myself permission to not be perfect was indescribable. With my death-grip of control released, I was finally able to give God control of our circumstances.

At around four months old, Coleman's first surgery was officially scheduled. As discussed at a follow-up urologist appointment, we knew to expect it to occur before his first birthday. The surgery was to correct congenital issues and was considered routine. This type of surgery was routine for other people's children and maybe the doctor, but for us, it was anything but.

We drove over early the day before the surgery to sightsee and take in some tourist attractions in New Orleans. The Aquarium of the Americas was our first stop, and Coleman's eyes lit up as he watched the sea horses gracefully swim around their tank of clear blue water. We took him to "eat" delicious New Orleans cuisine and to see the beautiful street art in Jackson Square. As we snuggled up under the covers at the adorable boutique hotel in the historic Garden District, we could no longer ignore the reason why we had traveled two hours away from home.

The hotel that tourists would book because of its location to must-see attractions, we booked because they offered a medical discount. We wouldn't awake early the next morning with excitement to eat breakfast at Mother's Restaurant (which I highly recommend if you are ever in New Orleans, by the way), but instead with great anxiety and a hungry child that couldn't have anything by mouth after midnight.

Although not ideal, we were making the best of the situation we were in. Intentionally finding joy in circumstances that threaten to steal it was going to be my normal outlook from this point on. All those negative emotions could so easily weigh me down and blind me to anything, but our current situation would not have lasting power over me. I would feel the feelings and cry the tears, but I would also laugh, joke, and celebrate the fact that we were given that opportunity to experience it in the first place. This shift would eventually help me find balance and happiness in the new life we had been given.

The morning of the surgery, we nervously handed our child to the medical staff and tried to make the time pass as quickly as possible. Although it felt like an eternity, our names were finally called to receive an update from the doctor. Sitting in a tiny little room, the doctor rushed in with a smile on his face and said that everything went great and Coleman was in recovery doing well. He had stitches, a skin graft, and a catheter so we would have to be trained on wound care before we headed home.

We had all survived, and it was such a relief. Although Coleman would require special care until the stitches dissolved and the catheter could be removed at his post-op appointment, he seemed unbothered by the surgery site. He ate and slept normally for the first couple of nights and we made sure to be proactive with his medicine to stay ahead of any pain. Other than one case of bladder spasms, you would have never known he had even had surgery by the way he looked and acted. Such a strong, brave little boy ready to face whatever came his way.

Little did we know at the time, that a great deal, in fact, would be coming his way. It has been said that what doesn't kill you, makes you stronger (4). You fight, survive, and move on. Each time, a little bit more prepared for the next fight. After what seems like an eternity of war that has left you feeling battle weary and scarred, sometimes you tend to wonder what it is that God is actually preparing us for in the future. Thankfully, our strength and perseverance come from Him, so regardless of the battles we face, the victory has already been won through Christ Jesus.

> **"The Lord is my strength and my song;**
> **he has become my salvation."**
> **Psalms 118:14 (ESV)**

Personal Reflections

What battles have you faced recently where you had to rely fully on God's strength to get you through? Have you ever had to amend your expectations of life in order to align yourself in God's will? If so, was it easy or difficult to do?

CHAPTER 7

Genetics and Assumptions

"To my brave, resilient little Coleman. Every child strug-gles. Every parent struggles. Challenges are nothing new in this world, and they are something we all must deal with. It is so tough to watch you be challenged with the things that come naturally or easily to other children. But where other parents might take for granted what their children have accomplished, we celebrate every milestone you reach like it is the most amazing thing that has ever happened in the history of the world! Because to us, it is."

LIFE WAS NEVER PROMISED to be easy. We all have struggles and trials that we face while trying to keep a semblance of holding it all together. Illness. Grief. Financial Struggles. Broken relationships. Unemployment.

We put on our brave faces and go through our dai-ly routine pretending not to be consumed with the constant worry running through our minds or the heavy burdens that weigh on our hearts. Unfortunately, life doesn't stop when times get tough. Bills still have to be paid, groceries bought, yards mowed, and every other minute detail of our day completed. How amazing would it be if we could just disappear for a bit to deal with the difficulties of life and then rejoin the masses after we have composed ourselves!?

So many times during Coleman's first year of life, people tried to build us up and support us with various clichés and uncomfortable encounters. Some folks polluted scripture and told us that God doesn't give us more than we can handle. Others shared the non-scriptural truth that God only gives special children to special parents. A thankfully small group of winners bypassed faith all together with their unwavering support. This support manifested itself in a few different ways including denying that he had any medical/developmental issues at all and telling us that they knew someone whose child had exactly what Coleman has and he or she turned out to be normal. In those exact words. Those exact words would bring such anger and ugliness from the bowels of my soul that I didn't even know I possessed.

Obviously, God had given me more than I could handle on my own because I wasn't really handling anything at all. I just appeared to be in control and taking care of business but inside, I was screaming, crying, and praying my way through each moment. I was a fragile hot mess sort-of held together by faith and caffeine. It didn't take much for me to crumble into a million pieces at that point of our journey, and it still doesn't on some days. I crumble because I am weak, but I rise again because He is strong.

God had also not given us Coleman because of our special skills and abilities as parents. God gave us Coleman in spite of who we are as people and parents. In spite of our selfishness, pride, disobedience, and brokenness. Maybe he will teach us something or grow us in some way spiritually, but his existence may have nothing to do with us at all. We are not doing anything special other than loving our child and meeting his needs. That is every parent's responsibility whether their child is neurotypical or developmentally delayed.

Unlicensed medical professionals would often voice their opinions of Coleman's case like it was going out of style. Incorporating and disguising their opinions within normal conversations, hoping to sneak in a diagnosis or treatment that would be the winning answer, as if he were a final Jeopardy clue. Doctors had still not given a genetic diagnosis, but the general public had given him hundreds. Some of the unsolicited treatment options we were told would have even made the old wives roll their eyes in disgust.

The "cradle cap" that he had since birth and everyone told us how to "cure" turned out to be a condition called aplasia cutis congenita that was harboring a staph infection. The staph infection led to abscesses that would explode with pus, and he would scream in agony if anyone or anything touched his scalp. The infection also traveled down to his recent surgery site and ate away the skin grafts, so he had to have another surgery to repair the damage. Scalp infections would eventually lead to another major surgery at age three and multiple trips to see infectious disease and dermatology specialists over the course of the next few years. What was dismissed by family and friends as no big deal, turned out to be a pretty huge deal.

Denial can be a disappointing coping mechanism, mainly because it doesn't ever let a person cope with reality. Scenarios are created in their minds that fit what they are willing to accept, and if the situation doesn't play along with their fantasy world, then it is completely ignored or manipulated into a more acceptable situation. In their minds, Coleman is just like every other kid without any medical or developmental conditions, and we, as his parents, are just trying to create issues for our own benefit.

By others trying to minimize my concerns, it made me use the little energy I had to argue that something was wrong with my child in order to be validated, heard, and taken seriously. It made me feel that deep down somewhere, I wanted him to be disabled and medically fragile, but the opposite was the truth. I just wanted unconditional love and support instead of opinions. It was such a frustrating, aggravating experience. I knew I would have to process my own acceptance of Coleman's condition, but it never occurred to me that I would also have to shoulder the responsibility of helping everyone else we know process it.

Eventually, there were no more excuses to explain delays or examples of "normal" children with his diagnoses. Then, the reality of Coleman had to sink in. Some took it well and embraced him fully while others disappeared from our lives forever. The folks that were left became our small, tightknit, supportive village.

I can't presume to understand God's plan for my son's life, and it is difficult to hear the reasons why we were blessed with such a unique child from others. If the intention is coming from a loving place, it is greatly appreciated, but words do matter and often, they are not helpful. Words can hurt in ways that the speaker will never be aware of, having been captured in the heart and mind of the listener. They are then remembered and ruminated on, causing the wound to deepen each time they are brought into focus. Some words will never be forgotten, but I know that I have been the speaker of such hurt when I didn't know how to empathize properly; therefore, I should offer grace and forgiveness to people who truly don't know what to say or how to be encouraging.

Coleman's six-month genetic follow-up appointment was soon approaching, and we were extremely anxious to see what the doctor had discovered since our initial virtual meeting in the NICU. The promises he made about researching day and night to discover Coleman's chromosomal disruption echoed in my mind as we prepared ourselves emotionally and mentally to receive answers. Of course, our child should be his main focus despite the fact that he sees thousands of kids from around the world. Coleman was our priority, and should be his, too.

We made sure to arrive early on the day of the appointment in anticipation of the large amount of paperwork that was required to be seen by medical professionals these days. Once the mound of forms was completed and turned in, we were told to be seated and that we would be called back shortly.

Just a couple of minutes later, the nurse came out and escorted us to a room. We were asked to give our complete family history . . . again. Then, we were asked questions about the pregnancy and delivery . . . again. I assumed that maybe the nurse hadn't read the chart prior to calling us back so she was just being thorough to ensure everything was documented. After three hours of answering questions that we had already answered during the NICU appointment and explaining everything that had occurred since, the doctor finally made his appearance. It became blatantly clear that the geneticist didn't remember Coleman, nor had he been spending his time researching, as promised. It was also obvious that he didn't even review the information that the nurse had just taken before coming into the room.

We just had a four-hour appointment with a specialist to be told that he didn't have any answers, and he would like to consult with his colleague before he decided on an action plan. He didn't even have any idea on what further testing he would want to run. I think we were more disappointed than angry. Disappointed because we still didn't have an idea of what was going on with our baby. We didn't know a prognosis or if we should ever have more children, and the unknown was the hardest thing to deal with. The one thing we were sure of after the appointment was that we needed to find a new doctor.

In a world of search engines and instantaneous answers, one would hope to just Google symptoms and immediately be given every bit of information imaginable. Since we had to wait two months before seeing the new geneticist, there was plenty of time to continue my personal research. This crusade had begun mere hours after Coleman's birth and would continue until we received a genetic diagnosis.

What started as innocent inquiries quickly became an obsession. Every free moment of my day and some of my nights were spent searching for syndromes or chromosome abnormalities that would explain his issues. The research helped me channel my anxiety and focus it on something I could control rather than the million things I couldn't. "What causes hypertelorism?" "What causes agenesis of the corpus callosum?" "What causes congenital deafness?" "What causes . . ." on down the list of Coleman's symptoms I would go. After researching each individually, I would then up the difficulty level and start searching for two at a time. Then, three. I just knew at some point I would come across a case study or parent's blog about a child that had everything he had, and then we would have our answers.

Although searching indiscriminately had the very real risk of creating more anxiety since most medical articles don't include the best-case scenarios for your reading enjoyment, it had the opposite effect on me. It was calming and therapeutic because I was able to separate myself and look at the information scientifically and not emotionally. I learned more during those months than I did in any college-level biology class. It was all so interesting and complex.

While I was working towards my Ph.D. in genetics from Google University, I realized some very useful tidbits of information. Basically, the science of genetics changes daily as new discoveries are made, so what you read today may not be true tomorrow. Also, there are an infinite number of disorders and syndromes that all have the same physical presentation and symptoms. I knew better than to show up at the new geneticist's office with a list of diagnoses I found online along with the corresponding tests I wanted to run to prove/disprove said disorders. I knew better, but it sure was tempting.

It was going to be good to start fresh with someone who had never laid eyes on Coleman and who didn't have any preconceived ideas of a cause. We needed this new doctor to think outside of the box because our boy definitely didn't conform to the norm. My prayer before we left to head to his appointment was that God would provide us some peace, whether it came from receiving answers or just in continuing in the unknown. I knew my current rate of trying to figure him out on my own couldn't continue indefinitely so at some point, I may have to face the fact that we would never know the reason.

The appointment with the new geneticist began with his genetic counselor taking our family pedigree. Since the family histories were included in the medical forms I had faxed to them weeks prior to the appointment, I was once again feeling like no one had even put forth the effort to look at Coleman's file. However, right away she started referencing details in it and knew a lot of it off the top of her head. At this point, we felt like we were where we needed to be.

After the counselor left, we spoke to a medical student and gave more details about Coleman's conditions. We arrived at 1:30 p.m., and at this point, it was already 3:45 p.m. Unlike the visit with the last geneticist, we were talking to medical personnel instead of being stuck in a room alone for two hours. During the consult, we found out that we were the only appointment for the afternoon, which meant the doctor was totally focused on us. He came in around 3:45 p.m. and started his physical examination. He explained everything he saw and used nonmedical terms so we could understand what he was talking about. Every few minutes, he would stop to ask us if we had any questions.

I wanted to jump up and give the doctor a hug, but I refrained because I am pretty sure that would have been a little creepy on my part. After the exam, the doctor and his counselors went out to discuss a few things and then returned to wrap up the appointment. By the quickness of their discussion, I figured that they probably had a few ideas already in mind before our visit and wanted to examine him before sharing anything with us. We were told that they really don't know for sure, but that the original genetic testing done at birth that came back normal didn't rule anything out except for the major defects. It was just a quick snapshot of the surface, but that there were several other tests that could zoom in and look at specific areas of genes. One of those tests, the SNP array, was what he wanted to run first. He said that Coleman exhibited many of the characteristics and medical issues that are associated with a chromosome 22q deletion, but the additional test would verify.

The SNP array would be run on a tissue sample taken while Coleman was under anesthesia because tissue cells are slower growing and slower dying than blood cells so they retain the genetic material longer. This type of test would make it easier for the lab to examine his genetic makeup and spot any inconsistencies. We were pleased to have an action plan instead of just saying we would watch him and see how he develops.

We left that appointment with hope and all the defeat from the previous months seemed to vanish. We would still have to wait a while to run the test because the doctor didn't want to put him under anesthesia and cut him any more than was necessary to obtain the tissue sample. Instead, we would wait for an upcoming scheduled surgery, either the second hypospadias repair or cochlear implantation, to remove the needed tissue. Someone was finally on our side and willing to fight along with us for answers, and it was the most reassuring feeling in the world.

"Blessed be the God and Father of our Lord Jesus Christ, the Father of mercies and God of all comfort, who comforts us in all our affliction, so that we may be able to comfort those who are in any affliction, with the comfort with which we ourselves are comforted by God."

2 Corinthians 1:3-4 (ESV)

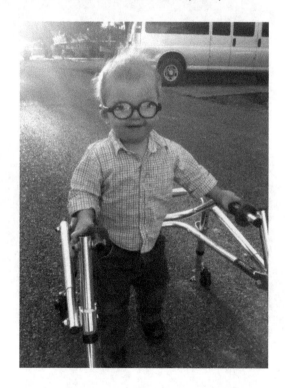

Personal Reflections

Have you ever been in a situation where you received unsolicited advice or opinions from others? How did it make you feel? How do you encourage others going through something you have never experienced personally? What are some scriptural truths that you find encouraging during life's difficulties?

CHAPTER 8

Born to be Different

"God made you different from the rest, my love. You aren't meant to blend in and conform, fading into the background. You are meant to stand out and be noticed. Hands flapping with excitement and happy squeals cutting through the silence of mediocrity. How boring life would be if you were just like everyone else! Your joy and laughter make even the toughest days better, and your sweet smile offers assurances that no challenge will ever be too big to conquer. Don't feel embarrassed or ashamed of who you are but confidently embrace your rareness, abilities, and talents. Be you so that the world can see Him."

SOCIETY HAS CRITERIA USED to measure the normalcy of individuals based on where they fit in amongst the majority. Whether it is your physical appearance, intelligence, or behavior, certain characteristics are deemed abnormal by these standards if they fall outside of the set limits. You may fall in the abnormal range in some areas but your average in other areas can bring you up to a level that is deemed acceptable by the masses.

The concept sounds incredibly harsh, but we are all guilty of judging others, in one way or another, based on our idea of normal. Maybe it is just because of flawed human nature, but the consequences of it can be detrimental. We create an environment of exclusion, whether intentional or unintentional, which means we minimize a person's worth based on something that is beyond their control.

As a parent of a child with multiple disabilities, exclusion means that he isn't good enough to attend the birthday parties of kids at his daycare. He isn't good enough to be in a classroom with his typically developing peers. He isn't good enough to participate in the Christmas play. He isn't good enough because he may take away from the experience of the "normal" kids and their families.

Anyone with manners wouldn't directly say that Coleman isn't good enough to participate, but nonverbal communication can also speak volumes. The looks of annoyed curiosity cut like knives when his squeals of excitement get blurted out during moments of reverence. The avoidance of eye contact by disapproving parents humiliates when his lack of impulse control causes him to push down or hit another child during fun activities. The expressions of pity project his differences on the big screen for all to see when his feeding difficulties prevent him from partaking in a holiday meal.

So where does he fit in? Does he fit in anywhere?

After he was born and we found out he was deaf, it was assumed by family, friends, and medical professionals alike that we would do the cochlear implant surgery when he turned a year old. The hospital audiologist provided us information on the process and informed us that the implant would fix the hearing issue so we could focus on his other challenges. It never occurred to me that this decision would end up being a very difficult one for us to make.

From the hearing perspective, folks assumed that the cochlear implant would cure Cole's deafness, and of course, believed there was no other option. It was a no-brainer, and their willingness to share this feedback was mostly unstifled. They appreciated the beauty and value in their own lives of being able to hear sounds and voices, and felt that everyone else, especially children, should be able to have the same experiences.

From the Deaf perspective, people felt their deafness wasn't a medical diagnosis to be cured, but a blessing that gave them access to an amazing culture and language. The cochlear implant is a very controversial topic within the Deaf community, and many believe that they shouldn't be forced upon a child when he or she has no choice. With the majority of deaf children being born to hearing parents, there is also a very real concern that the use of American Sign Language will dwindle as the next generation opts to use spoken language only. These opinions were passionately and proudly shared with us, sometimes to an extreme, just as the hearing opinions had been.

Both positions gave us a tremendous amount of information to consider, causing even more indecisiveness. In addition to the "to implant/not to implant" debate, we also had so many communication options to choose from. Among our communication choices were cued speech, spoken language, American Sign Language, Signing Exact English, and a total communication approach. Every choice had pros and cons when focusing specifically on Coleman's situation. Once again, Mike and I were completely overwhelmed because the "right choice" wasn't blatantly obvious.

Not knowing if he would be able to learn and understand sign language or physically use it as a form of communication due to his hand deformities, we still thought it was important for him to have access to language as early as possible. We started with baby sign language videos to learn how to communicate basic needs like "eat," "more," and "sleep." We would sign the basic vocabulary as best we could and tried to include it in our daily routine.

The awkwardness of trying to hold a baby in one arm and sign with the other while simultaneously doing some other task required of us made us feel like it would never become natural or easy. The desire to give up completely increased daily because it was all just too hard. Learning a new language is challenging enough, but we were also trying to teach it to a baby that stared blankly into space with no response or indication of understanding.

Not only was it difficult at home, but also when we went out in public. Fellow diners at restaurants or shoppers at the grocery store would gawk at us while we tried to communicate with our child. Even though, as an infant, he physically looked like every other baby, the signing gave away the fact that he was different. And people felt sorry for different because somewhere deep down in their hearts, different equaled something other than joy and happiness.

With the encouragement of some very good friends and mentors, we persevered and continued learning and teaching him the language. Neither the public's rudeness nor our own insecurities were going to keep us from giving our son access to one of his basic human rights.

With so many unknowns about the future and developmental delays, we decided that we wanted to do whatever we could to lessen at least one difficulty he faced. He was classified as Deaf Plus, which meant he was not only deaf but also had additional diagnoses. Those additional challenges significantly impacted his ability to encounter the world around him in a meaningful way. We wanted to offer him the highest quality of life, and through great amounts of prayer and research, we ultimately decided to proceed with cochlear implants as well as total communication.

Total communication wouldn't limit us to just one way of communicating with him but would expand our options to customize a plan that could meet his very complex, individual needs. As he grew and developed, the plan would be adjusted and adapted. American Sign Language would always be offered as a language option because the cultural aspect was important to us, but spoken language, augmentative/alternative communication devices, gestures and any other method that could enhance his ability to share his thoughts and feelings would also be supported. Coleman would ultimately be the one to choose how he wanted to communicate and that may vary from situation to situation based on his abilities.

He wasn't broken and a cochlear implant wouldn't "fix" or cure him. He was deaf and would always be deaf. If his cochlear implant processor breaks or when he takes them off at bedtime, he wouldn't be able to hear a peep. If he decides to not wear his processors when he gets older and fully immerses himself in Deaf Culture, we would support him completely. God created Coleman deaf, and we are very proud of that part of his identity. The cochlear implant would be just another tool to help him navigate his daily life.

Because no doctors locally performed cochlear implants at the time, we were referred to an Ear, Nose & Throat surgeon in New Orleans to do the preliminary testing and surgery. An audiologist, who was trained to map and program them once they were implanted, was also added to the team. The entire process required numerous appointments with both specialists before and after the surgery.

With all the research we had done on the surgery itself, we were completely taken aback at the first audiology appointment when we were told that there were several manufacturers of cochlear implants and different models of processors from each manufacturer.

It was like trying to pick out a new car. There were no five-star safety standards that vehicles are held to, but certain manufacturers had more recalls and device failures than others. Some companies had better customer service than others, which is important if you are needing replacement parts for an external processor. There were behind-the-ear, clip-on, and waterproof models as well as every color in the rainbow. If only we could have test driven them before having to choose, but alas, we didn't get that opportunity. After looking through catalogs, reading reviews online, and reaching out to other families, we made our choice.

At Coleman's pre-op appointment a couple of weeks before his surgery, we were patiently waiting in the exam room for the doctor. A young, blond woman in a white coat entered the room and began asking standard health-related questions, diligently noting our responses in the chart. She introduced herself as a medical student and mentioned how interested she was in his case. Her statement seemed odd because he wasn't the first person to ever get a cochlear implant and there wasn't anything extraordinary about his ears, nose, or throat. As our conversation deepened, we soon realized that she was referring to his genetic condition.

Coleman's physical features and medical history listed in his records had piqued her curiosity. Mike and

I told her that we didn't have an official diagnosis although his geneticist was hoping to get a tissue sample for the SNP test during one of his upcoming surgeries. Since the geneticist was at a different hospital, we were fairly certain that the administrative red tape would prevent it from occurring during the implant procedure. We wrapped up our chat just as the ENT entered the room for the exam. We assumed it would be the last we would hear from the sweet medical student from the Ukraine.

Surgery day was March 19, 2013. Both sets of grandparents and our neighbors (who are basically a third set of grandparents) all made the drive to New Orleans. Although he'd had surgery and been under anesthesia before, this was the biggest one to date. They would be shaving my precious baby's head and cutting it to place two small devices that would ultimately alter the only world he had ever known.

After hugs and some tears (from me, not Coleman), he was taken back to the operating room. A little over two hours later, the stoic lady sitting behind the mission control-style desk called our names for an update from the doctor. I rushed over so quickly that I became winded. Trying to play it cool and act like I was in better shape than what was blatantly apparent, I casually listened as the woman said everything was fine and moving along as expected. The news brought some relief, but we were still a long way from completion.

The surgery was scheduled to last approximately three hours, and he was taken back around 11:45 a.m. At 2:35 p.m., we got the update that the first implant was in, and he was still doing great. Our final update was around 4:45 p.m., letting us know that the surgery was finished and that a tissue sample for the SNP test had been successfully obtained during the procedure and sent to the lab for genetic analysis. It had taken longer than expected but not due to any major complications, and we would be getting to see him in recovery shortly.

Before the surgery, we had met with friends whose son had cochlear implants the previous year. At dinner, they answered all our questions and even had pictures so we would know what to expect with the recovery process. Mentally, I was prepared for the sight of Coleman laying groggily in some pain with a large bandage wrapped around his head. I was also prepared for the bloody nose that occurs as a side effect from the incisions.

What completely took me by surprise as I walked into the recovery area was the extremely, almost unrecognizably swollen child that was wheezing and struggling to let out raspy cries of pain. I felt almost weak at the sight of him, but knew he needed me to figure out how to comfort him. His eyes had swollen shut so not only was he deaf, but he was also temporarily blind. He must have been terrified, not knowing we were there with him the entire time.

Standing next to the monitors, the nurse studied them intently. She told us we could hold Coleman while she went to discuss his vitals with the doctor. The beginning pangs of panic started swirling deep in my stomach, and the feeling that had become so familiar in the NICU hit me again with overwhelming intensity. Once again, I felt like something was terribly wrong.

The nurse came in to tell us that the doctor wanted to admit him to the Pediatric Intensive Care Unit for observation because he was having some difficulty maintaining his oxygen levels. Even though it was explained that it was more than likely because he was intubated for so long and his respiratory system was just a little inflamed, I still jumped to the unsubstantiated conclusion that we might lose him. They also said that his extreme swelling was due to the I.V. fluids in surgery and they would be giving him a diuretic to help alleviate some of his discomfort.

Since only one parent could stay in the PICU, Mike told me to go back to the hotel room located at the far end of the hospital and rest. All my energy long ago drained from my body, I was too exhausted to argue with him. After tons of kisses to Coleman's inflated cheeks, I made my way through the winding hospital, through the hotel corridor, and arrived at our room. The ringing phone startled me awake hours later. It was Mike telling me how much better Coleman was feeling and that he would be moved to a regular room soon. Still wearing the wrinkled clothes from the day before that I had fallen asleep in, I rushed back to the PICU.

With all the swelling gone, he finally looked like our baby again. He was alert and happy to see Mommy and Daddy. Once he was transferred to the regular room and demonstrated he could hold down liquids, we were discharged to go home. Instead of driving the two hours back home, we stayed an extra night at the hotel so we could all get some much-needed rest.

The week after surgery, we were scheduled for his post-op checkup with the surgeon. The medical student that we had spoken to in pre-op stopped in to surprise us. She told us that she hadn't been able to get Coleman off her mind and had contacted his geneticist to discuss her opinions on his case. Medical releases had been signed so the doctors could discuss taking the tissue sample, and we knew there would be communication between the two. However, the fact that she had even thought about Coleman after meeting him the first time, much less took it upon herself to research and reach out to the geneticist was an incredible surprise. This overzealous medical student wanted to save the world (or at least help our family), and we couldn't have been more thankful. Once again, God's hand in our situation was evident.

As I pulled into the physical therapy clinic parking lot on the afternoon of April 5, 2013, for Coleman's weekly appointment, my cell phone rang. The number had a Baton Rouge area code, but it wasn't a number that I recognized. Hastily answering it while I gathered up our belongings to carry inside, my impatient tone reflected the thought that the person on the other end would be a telemarketer of some sort.

The friendly male voice was not trying to sell me a subscription to the latest money-making pyramid scheme, but instead wanted to give me the results of the SNP test. It wasn't a nurse or genetic counselor, but it was the doctor himself calling with the latest news. Knowing that conversational pleasantries would not be in my best interest at this moment, he quickly told me that the test had come back showing a chromosomal abnormality.

Mosaic chromosome 13q12.2-34 deletion. I wrote down as many of the numbers and letters as my mind would allow me to process, and I remember vividly thinking that I would just Google it later to get the specifics. I was certain that I had probably read something about it during my year long quest to find a diagnosis so it wouldn't be difficult to get information and connect with other families.

Before hanging up, the doctor mentioned that the only significant finding he had to share at this time was that Coleman's deletion contained a band that carried tumor suppressing genes. Medical journals indicated that there was a higher rate of eye cancer in children who were missing these genes. We would need to get in to see a pediatric ophthalmologist as soon as possible to monitor for retinoblastoma.

A peace rushed over me, and it felt as if a thousand-pound weight had been lifted from my shoulders. I would have thought that hearing something was wrong with my child's genes or that he was at higher risk of cancer would have thrown me into an emotional tailspin, but instead, the exact opposite had occurred. God had heard our pleas for answers, and He provided us with what our hearts longed for. We finally had a name for Coleman's condition. It was a rather long and complicated name that required tons of practice to recite by memory, but it was a name.

I grabbed Coleman and rushed him into the therapy appointment that we were now running late for. Explaining everything to his physical therapist, I told her I would be on my phone researching while they did his session. I started out by typing the entire deletion into the search engine and when no results were found, I shortened it a bit by removing the last set of numbers. This was my method until I was down to "chromosome 13q deletion." At last, a couple of links to resources popped up in my browser.

The truth slowly sunk in that his diagnosis wasn't a popular one. It wasn't one that had worldwide support groups, 5k-walks to raise money, or an awareness ribbon. It wouldn't be one that doctors or specialists knew much about, if they knew anything at all. It was rare which meant he was rare.

During some seasons, growth occurs slowly, almost unnoticeably over time while during others, it is like a seventh-grade growth spurt that seems to happen overnight. The first thirteen months of Coleman's life was a definite spurt. We had been empowered and equipped to fight for what we thought was right for our child, knowing that if it didn't work out like we had expected, we could alter the game plan and try something new. There was a huge learning curve with every decision we would make because he is unlike any other child ever born.

He is different. He is special. He is Coleman.

"Do not be conformed to this world, but be transformed by the renewal of your mind, that by testing you may discern what is the will of God, what is good and acceptable and perfect."

Romans 12:2 (ESV)

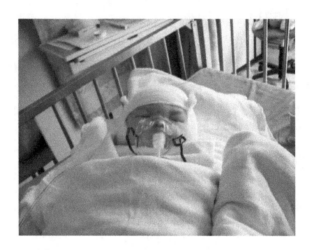

Personal Reflections

Have you ever experienced a time when you stood out from those around you? Has peer pressure ever caused you to try to fit in with the crowd or are you comfortable going against the flow? In addition to Romans 12:2, what other scriptures remind us, as Christians, to be different from the world?

· CHAPTER 9 ·

Ain't Misbehavin'

"You are just a little boy in this big ol' world, trying your best to survive. It can be scary and too much to deal with for adults at times, so I can only imagine how you feel. When life gets overwhelming and your emotions overflow, know that we will always be here to comfort and support you. We will be brave together, and I will prepare you, as best I can, to confidently face what lies ahead. Your bear hugs and toothless smiles remind me that bad days don't last forever, and tomorrow holds the promise of a fresh start."

THE OLD ADAGE GOES "actions speak louder than words;" but when you have no words at your disposal, actions are the only way to communicate your feelings and needs. Your actions are meaningful and are fueled by your desire to inform and educate those around you. Your behavior becomes a fight-or-flight response, a defense mechanism that tells others to beware when you are overwhelmed by your surroundings and emotions. This is Coleman's reality. Processing and interpreting must be done slowly and in small increments, so when life throws speedballs at him, he swings away blindly, trying to avoid being hit by the pitch. In self-defense and for self-preservation, he lashes out, just trying to survive.

Coleman's perspective of the world has always perplexed me, and I would love to see what he sees so clearly and feel what he feels so deeply. To be in his little mind for just five minutes would probably be the biggest adventure of my life. His actions don't always make sense to someone watching from the outside of his brain, and to try to explain them using a "normalized" vantage point, is impossible.

Behavior tends to be a major challenge when a child has cognitive delays, anxiety, ADHD, sensory processing disorder, and autism. Through varying combinations of specialists, therapists, medications, and natural supplements, we are on an endless search for the exact regimen that will alleviate some of the effects of the diagnoses.

When Coleman was younger, there wasn't much difference between his behavior and other toddlers. All toddlers have impulse control issues, overact when they don't get their way, and tend to physically respond when their space is invaded. This is a natural stage of development, and with a little guidance and positive discipline techniques, the neurotypical child learns how to appropriately interact with peers and adults.

As he grew older and started school, it was becoming obvious that his behavior was becoming more of an issue. The preschool class at the school he attended fit his needs perfectly because it was a flexible, fun environment with learning centers and hands-on experiences. When he was promoted to first grade, he was unable to live up to the expectation of sitting at a desk quietly and completing busy work for extended periods of time. His failure to meet this expectation would ultimately be one of the excuses that the school used to request a transfer back to his home district.

Once we received a formal autism diagnosis by a developmental pediatrician, we decided to enroll Coleman in Applied Behavior Analysis (ABA) therapy. ABA has been clinically proven to help children with autism by analyzing why negative behaviors occur and then teaching the children appropriate replacement behaviors. Communication and social skills can also be improved with ABA. Although not for every child on the spectrum, we felt that it would benefit Coleman tremendously. Unfortunately, due to the high rate of autism, these services were in high demand and most places had extremely long waiting lists.

After a year of impatiently waiting for an opening, Coleman was finally able to start therapy in August of 2018. The therapists and technicians assigned to him developed a plan to address Coleman's undesirable behaviors such as aggression, meltdowns, elopement, and noncompliance. My optimism skyrocketed, and I had the highest hopes that the issues would be magically erased within a few sessions. How absurd and unrealistic it was for me to dream of such an outcome, but it made me feel better temporarily and gave me hope that in the future, he will be able to overcome the ones that significantly impact his quality of life.

Until he can effectively cope with his stressors, our day-to-day lives involve extensive hypervigilance in preventing, distracting, and redirecting Coleman as to avoid any possible situations that could cause a meltdown, aggression, or injury. It. Is. Exhausting.

Studies have shown that certain parents of children with autism have stress levels comparable to combat soldiers (5), and I would have to agree whole-heartedly. Although it obviously depends on specific situations, the stress response and toll it takes on the body is very similar. The mental and physical energy parents utilize to mitigate risks while performing tasks that typical families do automatically is unfathomable. We are always on alert. Always looking for dangers or things that will set him off. Always on duty with no break in sight.

Sometimes I long for the ability to just show up. Show up to appointments, events, functions and a million other places that families go without having to overanalyze every possible scenario that might trigger my child's behavior. This isn't the "Will my child behave age appropriately while we attend X,Y,Z event?"-type of concern. It involves so much more than that, and sometimes it is a matter of life or death.

My sweet and affectionate child can have really tough moments when he doesn't know how to deal with everything he is feeling inside. People see this behavior and use it to label Coleman. I see Coleman and label the behavior. The behavior is frustrating and unpredictable. The behavior alienates his friends. The behavior is a small slice in a large pie of loving, kind, silly behaviors. It is a piece or part of what he does, not who he is. He is Coleman. The behavior is hitting, throwing himself on the ground in a meltdown, and running away. There is a huge, important difference, and I wish everyone could make that differentiation.

Where there is one negative reaction from him, there are hundreds of joyful, happy ones. Hands are not for hitting. They are for telling me he loves me. They are for holding mine as we walk down the street. They are for freely flapping and waving to show his excitement. They are for me to wipe clean if he gets a drop of food on them. They are for gently petting his puppy dog. They are for strategically choosing his favorite airplane videos on YouTube. Hands are not for hitting, but sometimes they do. Sometimes the world is too overwhelming, and the only way to cope is to hit and push everything and everyone out of his way.

Behavior in complex individuals like our son can be unpredictable, disruptive, and uncontrollable. The hardest part of this aspect of our lives is that Coleman wants to be around his peers and do what they are doing but he gets so easily overstimulated. We are walking a wobbly tightrope of inclusion and isolation.

Stares. Judgmental words. Whispers of disapproval.

I have witnessed them all but in the middle of the chaos, my focus is on helping Coleman and not everyone else's perception of him or our family. Let them stare. Let them gasp. Let them openly judge our parenting. It is not my place to convince them otherwise. I can teach, advocate, and raise awareness, but I can't change people's hearts or perceptions and I have to stop trying to.

The easiest thing to do would be to stay home and shield Coleman from the cruelty that lurks outside instead of exposing him to situations he may or may not be able to handle. But then everyone would miss all the wonderful things he offers, which brighten even the darkest of days.

Overreaction on Aisle 7

Grocery shopping has always been a challenge for us as it is for most families with young children. Where others deal with kids wanting every toy they see or candy in the checkout lane, our family had to deal with a much different issue. For years, I couldn't place any item in the large section of the grocery cart if Coleman was with me. I would have to precariously stack my items in the smaller section at the front where the toddlers usually sit or, if it was too big to fit there, it had to be placed underneath the cart. The meltdown that ensued if I forgot the rules of engagement would be epic and would bring our shopping trip to an abrupt end. The screams and crying could be heard throughout the store, and people would turn and watch to see what I was doing to hurt my child. All because I put an item in the grocery cart where items are supposed to be placed.

Party Pooper

Anytime Coleman is invited to a birthday party, my heart instantly fills with fear. What excuse could I come up with to not attend without having to lie? On one hand, I am so excited because a lot of kids with special needs aren't invited to parties. These invitations are coming from people that see Coleman, love him, and want to include him in their special day. On the other hand, experiences at birthday parties (including his own) have been mostly on the not-so-positive end of the behavior spectrum so I am hesitant to expose him to a known trigger. We finally decided to stop doing birthday parties altogether. We are now open and honest about why we are unable to attend other parties, and I have accepted the fact that my child doesn't need a Pinterest-perfect, stress-inducing party of his own. Our celebrations have evolved into family dinners at the local Mexican restaurant because that is what brings him the utmost happiness.

Anxiety Disguised
Santa Claus. The Easter Bunny. Sports Mascots. Clowns. All these costumed individuals evoke intense terror in our eight-year-old son. We have had to completely leave buildings and arenas because someone in a costume entered our general vicinity. We steer clear of shopping malls, especially around the holidays when the live Santa Claus or Easter Bunny is waiting to pose for overpriced photographs. Coleman shakes uncontrollably in fear while trying to escape by any means necessary. Climbing over rails, running through

emergency exits, and bumping into anyone or anything in his way, all while causing quite a noisy commotion in the process.

A Horse is a Horse, Of Course, but Also a Source of Panic!

Routine is very important to Coleman, so if anything deviates from it, he gets overwhelmed. When he gets overwhelmed, all of us get overwhelmed. We try to keep a steady schedule and anytime we know there will be an unfamiliar experience or situation, we try to practice the scenario ahead of time. One such example was when Coleman's physical therapist recommended hippotherapy.

Hippotherapy is basically physical therapy done on horseback. The horse's gait so closely mimics the way a human pelvis moves that riding a horse stimulates and strengthens the specific muscles and nerves needed to walk independently. The horse becomes a template and teaches the rider's body how to move correctly. Hippotherapy also improves balance issues and core strength, which we knew would be big obstacles that Cole would have to overcome.

There was one problem, however, with Coleman starting this type of therapy. He was TERRIFIED of horses. The first time we took him to the horse arena, he screamed as loud as he could until we got back into the safety of the vehicle. We knew we had to desensitize him and build his confidence, and that it wasn't going to happen overnight. We started out by walking up to the gate of the arena while holding Coleman in our arms. The horses were at the opposite end of it so he could see them, but they did not appear threatening. The next step was to go inside the arena but still a decent distance from the horses. We then got to the point where we could stand next to the horse with Coleman without him objecting. The final step was to pass him over the top of the horse to another person, mimicking how it would feel when we would place him on top to ride. At last, Cole was finally brave enough to sit on the horse without shedding a tear. The entire process took roughly six months and involved weekly trips to the arena as we progressed through each step. As difficult as it was during the beginning, it ultimately led to the beautiful friendship between Coleman and a horse named Rose.

Tornado Warning

Debris scattered all over the ground with shards of broken glass reflecting in the light. Sentimental mementoes forever lost along with family photos and décor that graced the walls of our home. I'm not describing the aftermath of a devastating natural disaster but rather the destruction that has occurred at the hands of our young son. Like a tense scene right out of the movie Twister, Coleman rips and roars through places with no regard for who or what he runs into.

His mood isn't always a predictor of when this behavior will occur. Sometimes he is extremely happy and just needs an outlet for the excess energy. At other times, he is upset and angry and uses the nearest object to communicate his growing frustration. Whatever causes the lack of impulse control, it is definitely the reason why we can't have nice things (just kidding, sort of).

Coleman is a sensory seeker. His body's ability to sense certain movements as well as spatial orientation is limited so he compensates by seeking opportunities to receive that normal sensory input. We have swings and trampolines both big and small to help him regulate in constructive ways but sometimes he needs the feedback before he is able to access these tools.

During particularly wild periods, our living room resembles a WWE wrestling ring with anyone inside being subjected to "Stone Cold" Steve Austin's signature Stunner move. If you are lucky enough to not get choke slammed, you may get a surprise push from behind with such force that you lose your balance or worse.

Chairs and barstools are knocked over and tossed almost daily. A few window panes and table tops have been replaced over the years. TV screens have been damaged by thrown items and almost every toy Coleman has ever possessed has been broken at some point. It can be frustrating and scary and exhausting. I'm constantly cleaning up and super gluing pieces back together.

Over the years, the decorations in our home have transitioned into more durable and less sentimental items as a way to protect Coleman's safety as well as priceless heirlooms. One day, I will be able to set out Mike's grandmother's porcelain Christmas village without fear of the village's total and ultimate demise. But not today. Today, we will make our home Coleman's home, too. A place where he can feel, spin, jump, push, and throw without fear of judgement.

Although I joke when describing Coleman's behavior in terms of the Fujita Scale which classifies tornadoes based on the death and destruction they leave in their aftermath, Coleman's sensory issues are anything but a laughing matter. We try to address these difficult behaviors and redirect into less harmful and damaging ones, but if I talk to you and tell you that he is a F5 on any particular day, please send backup ASAP to help a tired momma out!

The Art of Escape
Because of Coleman's inability to understand danger, we also have a heightened sense of awareness for

possible threats that could severely hurt or kill him. It is like having to baby proof the world for a mobile eight-year-old. What appears to be extreme overprotective parents on the surface is really a life or death necessity. As he gets older and develops new skills, we have had to adapt our strategies to keep him safe.

Stories in the news are ripe with children with autism going missing only to be found days later lifeless at the bottom of ponds or rivers. Elopement is a huge concern for parents of children on the spectrum as well as their children's increased attraction to bodies of water. It literally only takes a second for something like this to happen. No one can be on alert 24/7 without getting distracted. It is impossible, yet we are required to do it.

Coleman has never really eloped to get away from us. His motivation to elope is to get to something he desires, and once he does, he stops running. If our car is parked on the other side of the lot, Coleman takes off running, zoned into his final destination, oblivious to any traffic or other dangers that stand in the way. He is such a fast runner that, even if you are standing right next to him, it is still a challenge to prevent him from taking off. Luckily, we can usually predict when these behaviors will occur, so we can implement precautions.

Our biggest fear isn't really that Coleman will get out of our house and flee, but rather, he would escape to go on adventures, not being aware of the dangers lurking outside. Because of his fine motor deficits, we have been lucky that it took so long for him to be able to turn knobs and unlock doors. However, when he did figure it out, we quickly realized that something had to be done to control his newfound independence. I couldn't even go to the restroom alone for fear he would dart out of the door if I took my eyes off him. Although he doesn't understand dangers, he does understand fully when to take advantage of a situation to get what he wants. Mom being in the other room would be the perfect opportunity to pull off a disappearing act.

We have tried doorknob covers and other devices that worked for a bit until he adapted and perfected his methods of escape. Our current fix is a handy little door latch mounted high above Coleman's head and out of reach. It has kept him safe, that is, until he figures out how to climb up and unlock it. Trying to stay one step ahead is the name of the game, but the game doesn't come with any instructions. It is trial and error while praying the error doesn't result in injury or death.

All these behaviors are extremely challenging, but they don't detract from Coleman's value as a human being. He isn't trying to misbehave or overact. He isn't being mean or bullying. He is a little boy navigating a scary world to the best of his ability. As his parents, we will teach him how to overcome his fears and show him better ways to cope with emotions. And if he fails, we will hold him tight, wipe his tears, and try again tomorrow.

> ""The steadfast love of the Lord never ceases; His mercies never come to an end; they are new every morning; great is your faithfulness."
> Lamentations 3:22-23 (ESV)

Personal Reflections

What strategies do you use to get through bad days? Does knowing that God's love for us is unchanging, even in our failures, provide you comfort? What emotions do you have difficulty controlling? List triggers for these emotions and ways you can avoid or lessen your response to them.

CHAPTER 10

Too Cool for School?

"Sometimes people won't think you are capable. Sometimes they will focus only on what you can't do instead of seeing your potential. Let them think what they want to because we know the truth. You have so many wonderful qualities, and your desire to learn is your driving force. I see you watching and taking in everything around you. Like a sponge, you soak it all up, adding to the information already consumed. Just because you don't always show us doesn't mean you don't understand. We all learn in different ways and at different speeds, but remember, my love, you are smart, and you can do anything you put your mind to."

AS THE ADVOCATE FOR my child with disabilities, I have grown accustomed to fighting. Fighting against unfair medical practices, insurance denials, public ignorance, and a multitude of other injustices that relate to Coleman's care. The fight isn't always easy, but I try to speak with the patience and kindness of Jesus in the middle of whatever conflict we are facing. I try my hardest, but I don't succeed in those situations when my humanness gets the best of me and comes raging forth from my lips.

Schools should be the one place where parents don't need to fight for services, yet they are the one place where parents must fight the hardest. It can be incredibly frustrating and dispiriting when the very institutions that are required by federal law to have your child's best interest at heart fail them miserably.

When Coleman aged out of early intervention services at three, it was decided that he would attend a school in a neighboring district because it housed the deaf education program. In order to maximize services for the deaf students in the area, several districts paid into the consortium and would bus the students to the designated school where certified deaf educators, interpreters, speech therapists and audiologists were employed. This felt like the right environment for him to be around other deaf or hard of hearing children while being exposed to signed and spoken language. He would also have the opportunity to be mainstreamed into classes with students who were very familiar with deafness, cochlear implants, and sign language.

Transitioning from daycare to school was a terrifying prospect as my baby wouldn't be considered a baby anymore. Only big boys go to school but our big boy wasn't potty-trained and couldn't eat solid foods yet. Would they care for him like he needed or would he be neglected and considered a burden? He would also be riding a bus because his school was nowhere near my route to work, and since Mike worked in the aviation industry, he was always traveling away from home. The thought of putting Coleman, who was nonverbal and had limited communication through sign language, on a bus with strangers to be driven to school and back every day did not evoke positive feelings.

Once all the preliminary testing was complete, we scheduled his first I.E.P meeting. I.E.P. is an abbreviation for Individualized Education Plan, and the meetings usually include every one that will provide services to the student (regular education teacher, special education teacher, occupational therapist, physical therapist, speech therapist, audiologist, adaptive physical education teacher, assistive technology specialist) as well as representatives from the school administration and school district special education department. With students like Coleman, there was rarely a room large enough that could comfortably accommodate a crowd this size, so it was always overcrowded and stuffy.

Having heard horror stories from other parents about I.E.P. meetings, I wanted to be as prepared as possible. I viewed it as war, and every five-star general had a strategy in place before a battle began. Signing up for every training session available in person and online, I learned as much as possible about the process. I had binders full of notes and examples of achievable goals highlighted for easy reference. I made introduction sheets with information about Coleman to share with the team and listed out all my parent concerns so I wouldn't forget them if things got heated. Preparing for any possible pushback, I practiced and perfected my responses in a way that supported my cause. It was finally time to face the enemy and show them what kind of warrior we had inside us.

Upon our arrival, the atmosphere wasn't what I was expecting. Everyone was sitting around the conference table, relaxed and smiling. They introduced themselves one by one as I diligently worked to impress their names into my long-term memory. No one seemed out to attack us or prevent my son from receiving the services he needed. Instead, it was quite the opposite. Each team member offered up suggestions that they thought Coleman would benefit from while addressing our parent concerns. The goals they set were realistic and attainable, and it was obvious that they wanted him to succeed.

Our first I.E.P. meeting experience had me thinking that every negative comment I had previously heard had come from overly dramatic parents who didn't get their way. If this was as bad as it got, we would have nothing to worry about. Our false sense of security made us hopeful that all school systems prioritize their students' needs above everything else.

Coleman stayed in the Pre-K self-contained deaf education setting until he aged out at six. He showed such progress during those three years, and the teachers he had were wonderful. Their approach always revolved around his strengths and how they could help him learn. We entrusted them with our child, and they nurtured him like their own.

The honeymoon phase of educational bliss would end shortly after he started first grade. He was still in the deaf education program but was moved up to a classroom that housed kids ranging from first to fifth grade, all with different learning abilities. One certified teacher of the deaf would have him in the morning for certain subjects, and then another certified teacher of the deaf would have him in the afternoon for the remaining subjects.

School began a few days later and all seemed to be going smoothly. His school-issued agenda was sent home nightly and the section designated for teacher feedback was blank. Every conversation that I had with the teachers never indicated that there were any major issues or concerns. Multiple times, I asked to be informed if there were any behavioral or learning issues so we could schedule a meeting to address them but was told nothing.

At the beginning of September, after several weeks of school, we received an I.E.P. meeting notification letter ten days prior to the meeting date as required by law. My initial reaction was that the teachers have had time to get to know Coleman and wanted to tweak the existing goals to fit his needs. Since there had not been any feedback regarding other concerns, I assumed the meeting would go as smoothly and positively as all the other ones.

The mood in the room was heavy and awkward, however, which starkly contrasted our previous gatherings. As we stared at all the familiar faces surrounding us, no one seemed to make eye contact. In addition to the current school and district representatives, there was also a representative from our home district. This didn't raise any immediate concerns because she had attended I.E.P. meetings in the past.

The meeting began with the group listening to parents' concerns, all of which had been communicated before but were repeated so they could be included in the current document. After we had finished our part, the specialists, teachers, and therapists went one by one listing everything that Coleman was unable to accomplish compared to his goals. Even more disturbing was the fact that they also shared every negative behavior he had shown while in their care.

Only one team member had anything positive to say about his progress. His adaptive P.E. teacher shared her excitement about his gross motor skills and how he frequently communicated with her in sign language. She even shared how he played appropriately with his peers and would even take turns during activities. Unfortunately, she couldn't stay in the meeting long because she had to go teach a class. Our only ally at the school had left us alone with the vultures who were waiting to pick us apart.

After everyone had given their reports, the principal decided to make her closing argument. Although we were in a conference room at a school, it felt more like a courtroom where our son was on trial for something that he was innocent of, and he didn't have an attorney to help plead his case. The principal laid a file on the table and slowly opened it up to reveal evidence of

Coleman's inability. We were told that the other children in the deaf education program at the school were all on the LEAP track, and "obviously, Coleman is not."

Apparently, his only value to the program would be his contribution to the standardized testing scores that influenced teacher salaries and school funding. We were told that there was no alternative track or curriculum through the consortium for students with disabilities beyond deafness.

As I looked down at the scribbles that Coleman had made on the worksheet, all that I could see was how miraculous it was that he was even able to hold a pencil and make those marks considering his diagnosis. My blood pressure began to rise, and anger started to consume me. Obviously, I live with my child and know what his limitations are, so I did not need a so-called professional to show me proof that my son was delayed.

After the principal finished talking, the district's special education supervisor took over and asked our home district's supervisor what they would be able to provide for Coleman and when we could make the transition. Mike and I were in complete shock. Even with all the negativity, it never crossed our minds that they were trying to get rid of him until we heard the last statement.

At this point, almost everyone was in tears and talking about how much they would miss him when he transferred to his new school. There really wasn't time to process what had just happened but luckily, we did not sign anything accepting the changes that had been proposed. We felt like Coleman's fate had been decided before we even showed up for the meeting, and everyone involved made sure to have the proof needed to back up their accusations. It seemed as if the transparency and cooperation that had once existed had been replaced with manipulation and deceit.

Being an advocate means knowing your child's rights and speaking up when those rights are violated. Despite all the training that I had attended and research I had done, the emotions that flooded over me during that meeting muted my voice and created uncertainty within my mind. I knew deep down what they were doing wasn't right, but I couldn't coherently verbalize why.

The events of that day didn't really sink in until we got home and started discussing it further. My heart was broken thinking about all the changes that Coleman would have to face, and my tears only stopped falling during the brief moments of sleep I was able to get that night. Once the emotional upset subsided, I needed answers. I reached out to educational support professionals, parents of children who were deaf with other disabilities that had gone through the program, teachers of the deaf in various online support groups, and the current district's special education supervisor who had facilitated the transfer. No one I spoke to, except for the supervisor, thought that the transfer was justifiable.

In my email to the supervisor, I asked for clarification on the reasoning behind their request. I also shared that initially during the meeting, Mike and I felt like we did not have a choice in the matter because we had been caught off guard. In response, we were told once again, but in more detail, that there was not a dual setting that included mild/moderate and deaf education certified teachers. The curriculum in the deaf education program was based on traditional standards, which provides students with the skills necessary to take the LEAP test and is taught by certified teachers of the deaf who aren't required to be special education certified.

The deafness was considered to be the "least of his worries" and wouldn't be addressed educationally until Coleman's other needs were met first. If he made progress and was deemed worthy enough to pass the LEAP test or be in the acceptable standard deviation range to grade level, then he could possibly be moved into the deaf education program again at that time.

The explanation seemed reasonable enough at first glance and satisfied my craving for more information temporarily. After considering it further over the next few days, things just did not seem to add up, and my intuition screamed to keep digging. My gut feelings have let me down in the past, but never, ever have they let me down regarding Coleman's well-being. I had to listen to my inner voice and continue searching for answers. Once again, I shared the response with my support network and once again, the feedback I received was overwhelmingly negative.

How could they justify separating out the cognitive/behavioral needs of students and the deaf education support, because they go hand-in-hand? Approximately 40 percent of children with hearing loss have additional developmental and/or medical needs (6). With the rate of autism being identified as 1 in 59 children by the CDC, all schools will be feeling the influx of students needing more mild/moderate and behavioral services. An entire population of deaf and hard of hearing children would be missing out on the specialized training of a teacher of the deaf because they had other diagnoses and challenges. It seemed so discriminatory.

I drafted another email but this time, I listed my demands. I asked that Coleman stay in his current placement until we were able to get all the information requested and could make an informed decision, not one based on a reaction to being ambushed.

In response to my requests, I was told that the supervisor would get back with me the following week. Maybe the delay was because he didn't have the answers or maybe he just didn't want a record of his responses, but ultimately, a second meeting was called to discuss my concerns further.

When the I.E.P. team met for the second time, the meeting was very similar to the first. My questions were answered a little more curtly, and everyone just kept repeating the same things over and over again. Their answers obviously weren't good enough the first time if I kept asking for clarification, but they had nothing more to add without conceding to the fact that they possibly had no legal ground to stand.

Mind you, none of the deaf education program limitations were ever communicated to us at any point during the previous three years he had been at the school. This lapse in communication was blamed on everyone that had been in the job positions before, and no responsibility was taken by the current participants. Their recommendations of the placement change were all under the pretense that it was what was best for Coleman.

At the close of the meeting, one of the team members told me not to worry about Coleman transitioning to a new school without having sign language support. It wouldn't be an issue because he doesn't communicate. That statement summed up the position of the entire team, with the exception of the A.P.E. teacher, and finally brought clarity to the situation for me.

They did not believe he was capable of learning and their expectations of him were almost nonexistent. From the school level all the way up to the district administration, it felt as if everyone had failed my child and were blaming him for not being successful. This was infuriating and heartbreaking all at the same time. We were prepared to proceed with formal complaints and legal action to show them that they were messing with the wrong family.

But then something happened that I wasn't expecting. I looked into the eyes of my precious, little boy and saw a child that used to love going to school but was now miserable. Although we were told he didn't communicate at school, his behavior indicated otherwise. He was frustrated and crying for help. Literally and figuratively. Although he is developmentally delayed, he is incredibly in-tune with how people treat him, and he knows when he is not wanted or valued. Was it the right decision to leave him in that environment where he had been written-off and where every single accommodation would be a struggle to get implemented?

Before making a final decision to transfer, I made an appointment to meet with the new school that Coleman would be attending to get a feel of what they were willing to offer him. The moment I stepped into the building, I could immediately sense that the atmosphere at the school was positive and encouraging. I was introduced to the group of educators, administrators, and therapists that would oversee his care. Coleman was with me so they could meet him in person instead of me trying to describe every little detail about him.

The general inquiry from the group was to find out how the school could meet his needs. "What can we do to make the transition easier and help him reach his fullest potential?" Those were the sweet, sweet words that echoed in my ears for days after our meeting.

Prayers, tears, deep discussions, and pros/cons lists consumed our time and attention for the next couple of weeks until we finally made up our minds. Although I wanted to fight to keep him in the deaf education setting, my heart knew that doing so would only make Coleman suffer. He would lose precious time in his window of development waiting on a broken system to accommodate him or he could move to a system that would meet him where he was and help him succeed. It was a no-brainer when we looked at it from that perspective.

The transition timeline was left up to us, and we decided to do it after the Christmas holidays. That meant that he would spend roughly two more months there before he changed schools. I asked if they would be willing to provide certain accommodations until the transition took place, and they eagerly agreed. If only they had been so eager to begin with, we could have avoided the entire situation. They were getting their desired outcome and had been successful in their efforts.

Coleman's bus driver got permission to continue driving him to his new school so he wouldn't have to have a new driver and aide, in addition to all the other changes. For a child that is autistic, change is a terrifying and often extremely overwhelming experience. By keeping one aspect the same, at least his entire world wouldn't be turned upside down. We will forever be grateful for this man's kindness and sacrifice to ensure Coleman had something familiar in all the confusion.

Even though it wasn't apparent at the time, and I can still feel anger when I let my thoughts linger on what happened, I can now clearly see God's divine purpose through the circumstances we faced. Coleman is thriving at his new school and has made leaps and bounds academically. He has a paraprofessional in his self-contained classroom who knows sign language and can communicate effectively with him. She also taught other teachers and students basic sign language so they could talk to Coleman. He adores her and runs to hug her at the beginning of each day.

The school district also provided him with access to a communication device so he can have an alternate method to express his wants and needs. There is daily feedback from the teachers about behavior and academics, and the I.E.P. meetings could be used as examples of how they should be done effectively. The goals and expectations for him are set high, and he is trying his best to reach them. Once again, school has become a place of joy and excitement.

There were so many lessons learned through this entire experience and each one has had a profound effect on me. Schools are run like businesses, and unfortunately, the students are the ones who suffer sometimes. It isn't always personal, even though it feels that way in the moment. Forgiveness is crucial to be able to make decisions based on what is right for your child and not on your pursuit of justice. Deciding not to fight isn't always acceptance of defeat, but rather not being willing to sacrifice success. Good people can handle situations poorly, but some people choose to be manipulative. Sometimes people count on your ignorance to work in their favor so educate yourself and don't ever be afraid to speak up.

The greatest lesson of all is that God's will isn't always the obvious path, and submitting to it may require you to walk through seasons of hurt to arrive where He wants you to be. He has plans for us, but those plans don't exempt us from the struggles that grow and transform us.

Sometimes the purpose of the pain isn't revealed to us immediately, years down the road or even on this side of eternity. Our Heavenly Father always keeps His word, and we can rest in knowing that by trusting Him fully, He will direct us with a loving, compassionate, and sometimes firm fatherly hand.

My pride and anger in seeking justice in the school situation was sinful. My self-righteous need to hold them accountable and make them suffer consequences for their actions clouded my ability to see that God was leading us to where Coleman would thrive and be valued as a person instead of a test score. At some point and unbeknownst to me, my crusade against the school district ultimately became a battle against God's perfect will. Trying to inflict as much pain as possible on the enemy, but I ended up only hurting myself.

Through meaningful prayer time and self-evaluation, I was able to let go of my vigilante desire for the outcome that I determined to be fair and surrender to the outcome God had determined to be best. Releasing the grip of control into the hands of a just and fair God freed me from the emotions that were holding me hostage. Only then could I see so clearly His mercy and grace.

> "Good and upright is the Lord; therefore he instructs sinners in the way. He leads the humble in what is right, and teaches the humble his way. All the paths of the Lord are steadfast love and faithfulness, for those who keep his covenant and his testimonies."
>
> **Psalm 25:8-10 (ESV)**

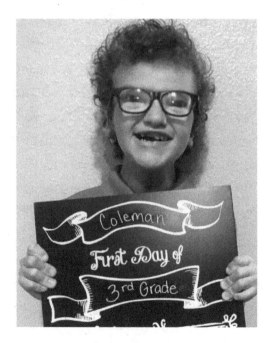

Personal Reflections

In what situations have you allowed your pride to cloud your view of God's plan for your life? Do you struggle with letting go of control and trusting God fully in certain areas? What does God's Word say about being humble, and how does that contrast the world's view of humility?

CHAPTER 11

Your Future's So Bright

"Thinking about how you will become a man in just a few short years has my heart filled with mixed emotions. I can't wait to see you grow and change, but a part of me selfishly wishes you would stay little for a bit longer. I think most moms feel that way from time to time. I am so proud of who you are becoming, and you never cease to amaze us with your accomplishments. Your witty sense of humor keeps us laughing, and your dance moves are the best I have ever seen! You make life more adventurous, entertaining, and fulfilling, and I am so thankful that we get to tag along with you on this journey. Just remember that no matter how grown you are, you will always be my baby boy."

WHAT WILL HAPPEN IN several years when Coleman outgrows the cuteness of childhood and transforms into a full-grown adult? His childlike mentality will remain but physically, he will appear to be a man. How will society accept an adult having a meltdown in public or stimming wildly when he gets overstimulated? It seems easier to accept or at least tolerate these behaviors in children because they are more common amongst the typically developing population, but no neurotypical adult is expected to behave in this manner. What will be the repercussions—public humiliation, police intervention, hospitalization, or worse?

I ask these questions in genuine fear because it is so scary to think that far into the future. The reality is that we, as special needs parents, must have some type of plan in place because our child's care and quality of life depend upon it. Planning on a life for Coleman without us is uncomfortable and emotional, but it is infinitely better than the unmentionable alternative.

Our little buddy is going to be our roommate for life. As other parents plan on sending their kids off to college at age eighteen, we will be going to court to declare him incompetent to care for himself. When our peers are becoming grandparents, we will still be deep in the trenches of our parenting responsibilities. When we reach retirement age and are ready to embark on new adventures, we will still be working in order to pay for Coleman's long-term care.

Although having a will and setting up a special needs trust isn't what average parents rank high on their priority list, it became number one for us. The thought of something happening to us and not having plans for Coleman's physical care haunted me. We had to choose someone as a guardian that would be able to carry the burden of caring for a special needs adult, both financially and emotionally. Our ultimate goal is to ensure he doesn't end up institutionalized somewhere or in a nursing home but rather with loving family that he is familiar with.

We must also make sure that we protect our financial assets so if we die, our insurance policies and any other money we have saved won't be used in calculating the amount of assistance he would receive through state and federal benefits. We wanted everything legally binding so there would be no confusion or dispute regarding our wishes for him and how to use the money we have saved for his care. This is heavy stuff for a young family to deal with, and it brings to light the realness of death.

As necessary as it is to plan and have everything in order financially and legally, I also have the reassurance that I don't need to fear what tomorrow will bring. By dwelling on and obsessing over what might happen, I miss out on the beautiful life we have been gifted today. My fear often consumes me during the quiet times when my mind has time to run free into the dark places, but I remind myself over and over that Jesus is the light and will illuminate all those formidable nooks and crannies I encounter.

Envisioning what we wanted our son's future to look like at this point looks very, very different than what I had expected those first few months after he was born. The unknowns early on prevented us from seeing the hope and opportunities that the future would hold, but now we have a more defined outlook. We want to offer Coleman as much independence as possible, so our focus is on helping him reach those custom goals instead of striving towards the standard-issued ones thrown at us by society.

We want him to be able to feed and dress himself. We want him to be potty-trained and be able to learn a skill that might lead to employment opportunities. We want him to be able to go into a store, pick out what he wants, and buy it. Even though he will probably not live by himself, it doesn't mean that he is not capable of having independence. We want him to feel pride in his accomplishments instead of always having to rely on others.

Coleman has always wanted to do things for himself. He would only tolerate minimal assistance from his therapists before getting frustrated and throwing a tantrum. His stubbornness and strong will made learning to stand, walk, and other important skills very difficult unless his therapists could come up with creative ways to distract him. As he has gotten older, he is now able to tell whoever is trying to help him to move out of the way, even if he has no clue what he is doing. I just wish that I could have an ounce of his confidence!

His strong determination propels him forward in learning new things and developing new skills. I know parents of typically developing children who wish their kids had half of the motivation to do things independently as Coleman does. As mentioned in the early chapter on behavior, sometimes his determination and strong will can manifest itself in negative ways, but there is so much positive that can come from it as well.

One morning after a few years of doing it for him, I handed Coleman his toothbrush and squeezed some toothpaste on top. I signed to him "brush teeth" to which he enthusiastically obliged. He had been watching and learning all aspects of his morning routine, just waiting for the chance to take over one or more of the responsibilities. After he had finished brushing that morning, he disappeared into the back of the house.

I wasn't sure if he had gone to find his beloved iPad or a matchbox car, but he soon re-appeared walking out of the master bathroom. What could he have been doing back there? From previous experiences, my first thought was that he was flushing a toy down the toilet or trying to overflow the sink so he could make big splashes. What I saw made my heart swell up with joy!! He had gone and placed his toothbrush upside down, next to mine in the holder. Because the holder was on the back of the sink, he had to stand on his tippy toes and stretch his arms super far to reach it.

So often in the hurriedness of our days, I unintentionally limited his ability to care for himself. Maybe I didn't have the patience to allow him the time to figure things out because we had somewhere to be by a certain time and it was just easier to do it myself. Maybe I was on autopilot, mindlessly going through the motions of getting everyone ready for their day that I didn't stop to think that he was completely capable of doing some of the tasks for himself. Whatever my reasoning was for being oblivious to his abilities, the sight of that little upside-down toothbrush completely changed my perspective.

I know it seems crazy and downright silly to think that a toothbrush could hold so much power. It was one moment that left an impression deep in my heart. Long before I felt God calling me to share our story, I had written down the word "upside-down toothbrush" in my journal. No other explanation was needed because those words help redirect my focus from just surviving the everyday, to helping Coleman thrive.

Once I knew my boy could put his toothbrush up after use, I felt he was unstoppable! I would go through every daily chore and routine making notes of what I could allow him to do independently and how I could modify it so he would be successful and safe.

Everyone that knows our family is well aware that I am no gourmet chef. I'm a master at heating up in the microwave and cooking recipes in a crockpot. One day, when Coleman walked up to the microwave and signed "food," I knew I needed to teach him some actual culinary skills. Mike could teach him the advanced stuff when he was home like making food taste delicious, but in the meantime, I could show him some fundamentals. Coleman and I made our grocery list for an easy-to-prepare meal and headed off to the local supermarket to learn basic shopping skills.

He absolutely loves the grocery store! Every time we drive by it, he squeals and signs for us to turn into the parking lot. He greets everyone he sees with a wave and a smile, and his buggy selection is very calculated based on standards he has set in his mind. After years of desensitization exercises and working with him, he is finally comfortable with us placing items inside the grocery cart. In fact, he wants to be the person who pushes the buggy and puts the groceries in it!

Other than a few displays knocked down and toes run over, he is rather good at navigating the aisles. He finds items that we have purchased before or that are familiar to him, and he adds them to our bounty. Even if we don't need more macaroni and cheese, we buy more macaroni and cheese. Once we have all the items we need plus some we don't, we head to the self-checkout lane.

Coleman takes items from the cart and slides them across the scanner (sometimes with minimal assistance) and then places them into a bag. When a bag gets full, he places it back into the cart and starts placing items into a new one. When it comes time to pay, he instinctively looks toward his mom for funds. I hand him my debit card and he knows just where it goes. We push the numbers together and he waits for the receipt to come flowing out of the machine. Off we head to the car feeling accomplished and successful, waving and smiling at everyone we pass.

Not all grocery shopping experiences are this easy and drama-free, but most of them are. We, of course, still have the occasional tantrums and meltdowns, but if I'm completely honest, I still have a few of those moments myself while shopping.

Once we arrive at home, he is an amazing helper at taking the groceries into the house. He grabs one bag at a time and will run inside to deposit it on the floor and be back at the car in the blink of an eye. Back and forth he goes until the trunk is completely empty. He then helps me put the groceries away, eager to begin cooking.

Our mini Gordon Ramsay starts chopping onions (with a butter knife for now), shaking salt and pepper to season the meat, stirring and mixing the sauce of the day, and adding it all to the pot. He checks the dish obsessively every few minutes to see if it is ready and waits patiently for it to cool so he can have a taste.

After the meal is consumed, somebody must do the dishes and lucky for me, it is Coleman. He loves rinsing off the plates, pots, and pans and placing them in the dishwasher. After the dishes, he cleans up any messes from dinner either on the table or himself. This inclusion in our daily activities gives him a sense of value and importance. Telling him he is important isn't nearly effective as showing him. Giving a thumbs-up and grinning ear-to-ear when he finishes a task lets us know that he understands how much the family truly needs him.

Obviously, we don't always follow the same routines or do the same activities just because Coleman expects us to or to prevent a major meltdown. He also must learn to have some flexibility when things don't go as planned, but we try to encourage him and allow him the opportunities to participate when we can.

A few years ago, I was diagnosed with a chronic illness, and it was another reminder for me of the importance of teaching Coleman self-sufficiency, to the greatest extent possible. Even if Mike and I don't tragically die in a terrible accident like our wills planned for, there may be circumstances and health issues that prevent us from taking care of his every need.

My condition causes higher susceptibility to infections and illnesses as well as extreme fatigue. Some days, taking a breath uses more energy than I think I can muster. I have palindromic rheumatism which has on occasion led me to be unable to use my feet and arms without excruciating pain. The combination of pain and fatigue contributes to brain fog that makes planning and carrying out the simplest task extremely difficult. There is a higher risk of certain cancers like lymphoma, so I have to have blood work every six months as a precaution.

Thankfully, there is a medication that I can take every three weeks that helps lessen the effects of the disease. The treatment, however, can cause additional negative side effects and involves me sticking myself with two needles into my upper thighs to infuse the medication. There are always blessings in every circumstance and being able to infuse at home at my own convenience is one of them. I can't imagine how difficult it would be to have to sit at a hospital for hours on end while trying to continue doing life.

The side effects can be terrible including horrendous headaches, gastrointestinal complications, fever, chills, and in rare occasions, acute aseptic meningitis. But these side effects are worth the risk to regain some degree of normalcy, and they usually subside two to three days after the infusion. A small price to pay for such a huge return.

The surprise diagnosis threw a wrench in the goals I had set for myself as a mom, employee, Christian, wife, volunteer, and individual. Adjusting these expectations was even harder of a process than I imagined. It felt so selfish. It felt like I was letting everyone down.

I grieved for who I was before, when taking a shower didn't exhaust me. When I was a reliable friend who didn't cancel at the last minute or have to plan time before commitments to make sure I could rest up so I would have the energy to go. Signing up to run a marathon and my body wouldn't give out during training a couple of weeks before the race. Not calling in sick on Monday because I overexerted myself by cleaning the house over the weekend. Being the award-winning mom who handmade Coleman's school Valentine's (because I truly enjoy crafting) instead of buying the generic ones from the store. That life was a good one. One I didn't appreciate until it wasn't mine anymore.

Once the mourning period was over, I was ready to adjust and accept my new way of life. Although many people aren't aware of my medical struggles, we have a small, wonderful support network that helps when I need them. Our sweet little boy knows when it is mommy's medicine time and always seems to give me just the right amount of snuggles.

I've let go of the truly nonessential parts that just consumed time and energy unnecessarily. I've not only let them go physically, but also emotionally. There is no room for worldly perfection anymore, and I am done trying to live up to that unachievable ideal I created.

I still run, but I listen to my body first and don't push myself. I still occasionally work on my art projects, but if they don't get done, it doesn't create anxiety. Some days my mom skills are amazing where the kid has eaten healthy things, made handprint crafts, practiced academic skills and had zero screen time. Other days, he literally plays on his iPad for hours so I can rest.

My spiritual life is affected by my illness as well. Sometimes, I can be at church serving and worshiping every time the door opens while other times, like flu season, I stay home and watch videos of services online to prevent exposure to illness.

My health challenges reinforced my drive to teach Coleman independence. How could I completely care for him when some days I can barely take care of myself? I pray that I will be healthy and able to provide for his needs for a long time, but I also want to try to equip him with the skills he will need in case I can't.

Looking towards the future also brings up the realization that our retirement years may not be filled with grandbabies and relaxing vacations. This saddens me a bit that Mike and I will still be parenting our child when others will be far removed from that season. The perseverance and patience needed to continue our current lifestyle for forty more years can seem impossible some days. It is in those moments when I know God hears my desperate pleas for reassurance because He allows me glimpses into what our lives may become.

Not literal glimpses of what lies ahead, but by using other families to show me that whatever plans He has in store for us, we will be able to push through the hard times and have a fulfilling, wonderful life. I see the elderly mom with her adult son with disabilities walking through the supermarket. She is patiently helping him navigate the aisle while holding his hand tightly, just as I do now with Coleman. Neither of them looks sad, depressed, or resentful because their lives aren't what they expected. She still has all the motherly love and affection she did when her son was a child, and he still looks up to her for guidance and instruction. It is a beautiful, rewarding relationship between parent and child that has continued getting stronger as the years passed by. How many parents wish that they could have that type of relationship with their grown children, and we are given that opportunity. An opportunity I wouldn't trade for anything in this world!

> **"But seek first the kingdom of God and his righteousness, and all these things will be added to you. Therefore do not be anxious about tomorrow, for tomorrow will be anxious for itself. Sufficient for the day is its own trouble."**
> **Matthew 6:33-34 (ESV)**

Personal Reflections

What aspect of your life frightens you when you think about the future? What steps can you take to stop worrying about future circumstances you can't control and start living in the present? How does knowing that, as Christians, we will have eternal life in Heaven help ease the anxiety of not knowing what heartache tomorrow will bring on earth?

CHAPTER 12

The Good Life

"As I reflect on the blessings God has given me each day, Coleman, you are at the top of my list. I'm thankful that I get the opportunity to be your momma, and the joy you bring me is immeasurable. Your natural optimism and precious giggles help me always find the good in life. The good that doesn't come from possessions or achievements, bringing only temporary happiness, but the everlasting goodness that is gifted from our Heavenly Father. Never, ever forget that you are precious in His sight and loved from the deepest part of our hearts."

MOMENTS BUILD UPON EACH other day after day, defining and sculpting our lives into what God crafted them to be all along. These brief periods of time can alter our very existence by changing our perspective and helping us see what we had been blind to before. Trauma can often lead us on undesirable paths as we try to search for ways to lessen the torment of events past, but only if we choose to ignore the infinite goodness of our Father.

During the darkest of times, I don't always remember to set my gaze on His grace and mercy because emotions overpower and overwhelm me. Absorbed in my own hurt, I move forward blindly trying to make sense of it all, oblivious that the suffering could result in something beautiful. The negative aspects of life seem to get captured and archived in my brain automatically, to be accessed with little to no effort.

The blessings, on the other hand, are easily missed, especially when they are hidden by a thick veil of pain. I have begun deliberately seeking and clinging to the indisputable reminders of His faithfulness and love. If I look with the right attitude and in the right direction, even during the greatest struggles of life, I should be able to find the Spirit-inspired joy that is promised. Although raising a special needs child has its fair share of heartbreak, hardship, exhaustion, and loneliness, it also comes with the greatest abundance of blessings.

Abounding in Love

Love. It is at the very root of our existence and the cornerstone of our faith. Love is more than words. It is action, sacrifice, forgiveness, grace, and healing all intertwined into a simply complexing phenomenon.

God encompasses all characteristics of unconditional, unselfish, agape-type love—love in its purest form—because He is love. God didn't need people but created us so that we could have a relationship with Him, and we are commanded to love Him in return with every fiber of our being (Mark 12). He sent His only son, who was innocent of every charge, to die on a cruel cross so that we may have life. This ultimate sacrifice atoning for our sins and all the wrongs we have done and will do so that we won't have to suffer the eternal consequences we deserve. God is never changing and always faithful. His love endures forever and ever (Psalm 107:1 and Psalm 136).

We are also called to love those around us, our fellow imperfect human beings, regardless of how hard it is to do so because of their behaviors or attitudes (Mark 12). We are shown how to conduct ourselves in a way that reveals the salvation-inspired love to the broken, lost world in 1 Corinthians 13. In summary, love is a big deal. The biggest deal. The one aspect of love that isn't guaranteed in our earthly relationships, however, is that it will be reciprocated in a way that is hoped for or expected.

When a child is nonverbal and is unable to properly show affection, a parent is often left craving some sort of response indicating their child understands the meaning of love. Hugs are rejected, words are ignored, and the attempts at making a normal human connection end in failure. Maybe they truly understand what love is, even more than we do, but they are just unable to express their understanding back to us.

Just because Coleman could not verbally say "I love you" didn't necessarily mean he had zero awareness of the unconditional love we had for him. The silence wasn't a life sentence because the possibility and hope he would be able to show and communicate his love for us remained. When my efforts were so brutally dismissed again and again, thinking on these truths helped ease the pain for a while, but my heart still ached for some type of response.

A few years ago, we received a call that my father-in-law had been unexpectedly hospitalized for a serious illness. Mike, Coleman, and I rushed to the hospital an hour and a half away so we could be in the presence of family. Everyone was anxious and upset, waiting for some news from the doctor. Crammed into an emergency triage room that was meant for only the patient and one other person, we made ourselves comfortable on the floor next to the bedside. Being together replaced any discomfort we were feeling and kept our minds off the germs that had made their home on the linoleum tiles we were now resting on.

The lights were dimmed, and everyone whispered in hushed tones to allow my father-in-law to rest peacefully. Almost instinctively, Mike signed "I Love You" to Coleman as he had done a million times before, but this time the outcome was very, very different. He picked his hands up off his lap and formed the sign that his dad had just modeled for him: "I Love You." With his little hands that were held in clenched fists for a majority of his first year; with his little fingers that didn't move independently and turned in unique directions; with his little smile spread across his face; Coleman actually told us that he loved us back. My insides turned to goo with indescribable happiness. The milestone we had been waiting on for so long had finally arrived, but ironically, it appeared during the saddest of circumstances.

Everyone's moods turned a little brighter and more optimistic at the sight of something we weren't sure we would ever witness. The light in the darkness. The joy in the pain. The reminder of hope when things feel hopeless.

Not long after he signed "I love you" at the hospital, Coleman learned how to give his famous bear hugs. It was the kind of hug that required skill and lots of space. It began when he started running full speed at you from across the room, with his arms spread wide. As he got within reach, he would jump with all his momentum and wrap his arms as tight as he could around your neck. You would have to brace yourself so as to not lose your balance and fall backwards onto the hard ground. You could feel a genuine connection every time he embraced you.

After he mastered the art of hugging, he began giving kisses when prompted. No one was exempt from the kisses, including dogs, baby dolls, and every human that requested one. The affection that was so desired and prayed for was morphing bit by bit into a fully spontaneous expression of love.

At age seven and a half, our sweet boy finally started communicating his love for us independently and in meaningful ways. As he casually walked by me on his way to play outside one day, he gently wrapped his arms around my leg, giving it a tight squeeze and a quick kiss. Before I could react, he dashed out the door to play on his swing set. To him, it was an insignificant gesture, but to me, it was a momentous occasion that I will hold in my heart forever.

Field of Dreams

Sports have always been a huge part of my life and are the center of most of my cherished childhood memories. My family played, watched, or attended games in whatever sport was in season at the time. As long back as I could remember, I had dreamed of being a sports mom. I looked forward to the opportunity to spend my Saturdays at a ballpark, arena, or field, cheering on my children with tremendous pride. I wanted to spend afternoons patiently teaching the fundamentals and skills and making sure they knew the importance of attending practice.

After Coleman was born, I felt like I might not ever have the chance to be the mom I had always dreamt of being. Not only was I grieving the dreams I had for him, but also for myself. One fall day, my brother contacted me about Coleman playing in an adaptive baseball program in my hometown. He wanted to be Coleman's "buddy" and assist him on the field. Although I was excited and optimistic that Coleman would enjoy it and do well, the games would be played three hours away every Saturday in September.

After deliberating over whether to register him or not, I decided that I could suck it up and commit to making the weekly trip. As inconvenient as it originally felt, I soon remembered that part of me that had yearned for this exact scenario for so long. My baby was going to be a baseball player, and I was going to be a baseball mom.

I went to several sporting goods stores searching for all the equipment that Coleman would need to be a star athlete. Glove. Bat. Bat bag. Cleats. Baseball pants and socks. A hundred dollars later, he was fully equipped for success and looking absolutely adorable.

The week before his first game, the coach sent me a message asking us to pick out a walk-up song for Coleman. This song would be played as he walked up to home plate each time it was his turn to bat. What might seem like an unimportant task to some, is actually an integral part of baseball. From t-ball all the way up to the major leagues, this song is extremely personal and well thought out. You don't just choose the first song you hear on the radio willy-nilly.

I began my extensive research which continued for days on end. I had to find the ideal song that represented Coleman's personality as well as the unique qualities about him. I was setting his baseball career up for failure if I didn't choose wisely and the pressure was enormous. I took this job very seriously, and ultimately found the perfect song.

How far I had come from the beginning of our journey! Early on, I was researching diagnoses and prognoses and now the most important aspect of my online searches revolved around finding music for my son to walk out to at a baseball game. The focus had shifted from searching for answers to living the life we were given to the fullest.

After playing his first season, Coleman's love of the game continued to grow. Our outings involve attending the local collegiate games during the summer as well as traveling to Chicago to watch the Cubs play at the historic Wrigley Field. Sharing in these experiences with Coleman has been a dream come true, and I am so thankful that God has given us the opportunity to make our own special family memories.

Go West, Young Man

Our family enjoys going on long, cross-country road trips, stopping at every historical marker and tourist attraction along the route. We started with a trip to Colorado when Coleman was one, and because he was such a great traveler, we decided to make it an annual tradition. Being in nature and around mountainous terrain that is nonexistent in Louisiana has such a healing effect on the mind and soul.

During the summer of 2016, on one of our many excursions, we decided to stop and tent camp at Yellowstone National Park in Wyoming. Hiking is a favorite activity of ours on vacation, and even though Coleman could walk by this point, he tired so easily that even the tiniest incline wore him out.

The night before we decided to tackle a trail, I read through the map given to us at the park entrance and selected one that I thought was compatible with our fitness and skill level. Not long after the sun rose the next morning, we headed out on our newest adventure. Although I had packed enough survival gear to make an eagle scout jealous, I forgot to grab the map with the name of the trail we were planning to hike.

After driving around the general vicinity of where I thought the trailhead was located, we finally saw the brown sign with "Mt. Washburn Trail" printed on it. I honestly could not remember the name of the original trail I had selected so I figured this one was as good as any. How difficult could it really be?

Mike strapped on the child backpack carrier we had purchased for such an occasion as this, and I carefully lowered our 4-year-old, 28-pound son into it and buckled him in. As we started up the trail, it quickly became obvious that it wasn't the easy, leisurely trail I had thought it to be, but instead was a moderately intense one that winded its way up to the very top of Mt. Washburn, a 10,000-foot mountain.

Moderate intensity doesn't sound too intimidating if you are relatively healthy and only carrying your own body weight. Add an additional thirty pounds and the effects of hiking at high-altitudes, and you have the perfect combination to induce extreme fatigue. Mike carried Coleman half-way up the 3-mile trail, and I carried him the rest of the way. Both of us huffing and puffing, desperately gasping for oxygen, all while trying to prove to the other that we were fine.

While it was my turn to carry the kid, we passed a group of college students walking back down the trail. Barely breaking a sweat, they were young, physically fit, and had reached the summit with ease. One of the men in the group shouted to us as he walked by, "You are the coolest parents ever. I wish my parents would have carried me up a mountain when I was a little kid."

It never had occurred to me before that all parents didn't strap their kids on their backs and hike up mountains. Maybe when they were babies some would wear them using a carrier or wrap, but most stopped when the child became more independent, mobile, and heavy. Although Coleman's small stature and low body weight always created difficulties in trying to clothe him, it now became an asset when being able to include him in our family activities for years to come.

I've heard about people having mountain top experiences throughout their Christian lives, but never did I expect to have one on a literal mountain. Maybe it was because I felt close to death with the lack of oxygen and dehydration, but God spoke to me that day through the college student we encountered. No, God wasn't telling me that I was the coolest mom ever, but instead, He was reminding me that my perspective of a situation determines my ability to see and appreciate His gifts. By fixating on the physical pain of carrying my child when others his age could walk and the distance we had left to travel before reaching a place of rest, I was missing the significance of the moment. No matter how bad life hurts, you can always, always find something to be grateful for.

Amazing Grace

Having been raised in church and saved in late childhood, I knew the importance of training up my own child in the ways of the Lord. Teaching, guiding, and showing him how to live in obedience. When Coleman was a baby, this was simple because all babies have limited understanding of spiritual matters. As he has gotten older, accomplishing this simple command has gotten more arduous and complex.

Introducing him to basic Biblical truths were complicated by difficult behaviors and limited communication. He was unable to respond in a way that indicated even the tiniest amount of understanding. It became discouraging and felt as if I was wasting my time trying to reach him.

Even in the church setting, he would mostly isolate himself from activities and lessons. Because cognitively he wasn't on the same level as his peers, he would attend the younger children's class in the hope that he would be more engaged and willing to participate. However, he would then get overstimulated and act aggressively due to anxiety.

The volunteers in the Children's Ministry as well as a few church leaders were all wonderful in their willingness to try new techniques and learn more sign language to make sure Coleman was included. If I was failing as a mother to reach him, how could I expect these individuals, who were already giving a tremendous amount of time and resources, to do even more for just one child. It seemed like it would be asking too much.

I started to understand why families that have children with disabilities often disappear from churches, not because of their falling away from faith, but because it is too hard to attend. What little energy I had left from the week of battling through crises, was usually gone by the time I could get dressed for Sunday morning service. I had nothing left to ensure Coleman's needs were met at the place that should be safe and comfortable. Asking for simple accommodations to help ease the burden was more than I could muster, even though I knew the church members would be eager to help.

Our pastor's wife asked me one day if I would be available to have dinner with her and a friend to discuss ways the church could meet the needs of families like ours. Her friend was the new Children's Ministry

Director for the state and also the father of a child with special needs. He was familiar with both sides of ministry-serving and receiving services.

As if God had shared all my secret concerns with this stranger before our meeting, the man addressed each one and validated the loneliness, isolation, discouragement I felt. He provided me with reading material and resources and offered to support our church in whatever direction we were led to proceed.

Through that conversation, my attitude began to change from utter defeat to true victory. From the devil's lies to God's promises. Only God knows what Coleman fully understands, but a lack of response shouldn't automatically be accepted as a lack of comprehension. Coleman should still be fed spiritually and even if accommodations are made only for him, he is worth the effort. Even if my attempts of reading the Bible, teaching him verses, and praying with him at home go mostly ignored, he is worth the effort. It is not my place to assume that growth isn't occurring.

I advocate and fight so hard for him educationally and medically; shouldn't I do the same for him spiritually? His spiritual well-being should be more important than any other goals we push to meet. In a world where nations allow babies' lives to be terminated before birth because of a suspected abnormality or disability, it is our responsibility to show that even though the world sees no value in them, to God, they are invaluable.

Whether or not he fully understands salvation or the intricacies of being a Christian, Coleman is loved immensely by his Creator and is important to the kingdom of God. Therefore, I must continue feeding him tidbits of truth, advocating for his spiritual needs, and finding meaningful ways to teach him about Jesus.

The first time I witnessed my son say the name of Jesus with his two hands, tears of joy poured out of my red, swollen eyes. Somewhere along the way, seeds had been planted, prayers had been answered, and a relationship with the Savior had begun. The gift of hope given where there was once none.

Life is good, friends, but not because of my possessions or anything I have done to make it that way. In fact, my broken parts try their hardest to focus on the struggle and pain. God purposefully created this life, and through His grace, I have every reason to rejoice and celebrate with every breath I take. Even in the storms and turbulent seas, I will praise Him and give thanks for the blessings He has bestowed.

""For by grace you have been saved through faith. And this is not your own doing; it is the gift of God, not a result of works, so that no one may boast. For we

are his workmanship, created in Christ
Jesus for good works, which God prepared beforehand, that we should walk
in them."

Ephesians 2:8-10 (ESV)

Personal Reflections

Is it hard for you to find joy in the difficult circumstances? How can you become intentional in searching for goodness in the tough times? List ten things you are grateful for during one of life's battles.

CHAPTER 13

The Lucky Ones

"The world sees your birth as a stroke of bad luck, something to be pitied because of the pieces that were not placed. Where others have no void, you are missing. What if you suffer and feel pain? What if you don't blend into the crowd or do what is expected? My dearest child, we don't believe in creation left to chance. A roll of the dice, odds in anyone's favor. You were formed and knitted together with the exact amount of fiber and thread to fulfill your purpose— nothing more desired, nothing less needed. We aren't tied to false reliance on coincidence or fortune or any other lie whispered throughout the generations. You are the handiwork of our Father God, and through you, evidence of His glory will be displayed to everyone you meet. You are a living reminder of God's faithfulness and love. Those that don't know the truth may look at our situation as unlucky, but we are actually the 'lucky ones.'"

"So now faith, hope, and love abide, these three; but the greatest of these is love."

1 Corinthians 13:13 (ESV)

Personal Reflections

As a living reminder of God's faithfulness and love, how will you encourage the brokenhearted with your story? Name three takeaways from your personal reflections that you hope to remember. How do you feel you have changed that will help you on your journey?

Personal Reflections

How did you feel at the beginning of your toughest trial? How do you feel now that you have made it through?

Your Personal Pages

Share what's on your heart and mind! You can also choose several scriptures to study and reflect on or write your testimony to share with others!

Your Personal Pages

Share what's on your heart and mind! You can also choose several scriptures to study and reflect on or write your testimony to share with others!

Bibliography

Kingsley, Emily Perl. *Welcome to Holland*. 1987. All rights reserved. Reprinted by permission of the author.

Louisiana State Legislature. State of Louisiana Act No. 653. 2016. http://legis.la.gov/Legis/BillInfo.aspx?i=56; http://ldh.la.gov/assets/oph/Center-PHCH/Center-PH/hearingspeechvision/LA_LAW.pdf

16personalities. *Advocate Personality: INFJ-A / INFJ-T (What's the Difference?)*. N.d. https://www.16personalities.com/infj-personality

Nietzsche, Friedrich Wilhelm, and Duncan Large. *Twilight of the idols, or, How to philosophize with a hammer*. Oxford: Oxford University Press. 1998.

Seltzer, Marsha Mailick et al. *Maternal cortisol levels and behavior problems in adolescents and adults with ASD*. Journal of Autism and Developmental Disorders vol. 40,4 (2010): 457-69. doi:10.1007/s10803-009-0887-0

Gallaudet Research Institute. *Annual Survey of Deaf and Hard of Hearing Children and Youth*. 2010.